READYMADE CENTURY

DIETER DANIELS

READYMADE CENTURY

SPECTOR BOOKS

"I'm not at all sure that the concept of the ready-made isn't the most important single idea to come out of my work." (Marcel Duchamp 1961)*

* Interview Kuh 1961, p. 92.

ACKNOWLEDGMENTS

During my work on this book I had the opportunity to present some of its theses in lectures and conferences. Thanks to Pia Müller-Tamm (Kunsthalle Karlsruhe), Katja Kwastek and Sven Lütticken (Vrije Universiteit Amsterdam in cooperation with Stedelijk Museum Amsterdam), Susanne M.I. Kaufmann (Staatsgalerie Stuttgart), Friedemann Malsch (Kunstmuseum Liechtenstein), Jacob Wamberg (Aarhus University) and the colleagues from the Kunstgeschichtliches Institut Frankfurt am Main in cooperation with Museum für Moderne Kunst Frankfurt for their invitations.

While writing this book I also curated the symposium *The Readymade Century* at the Haus der Kulturen der Welt Berlin (HKW), and I sincerely want to thank Bernd Scherer and Annette Bhagwati for this opportunity.

A very special thanks to Lars Blunck for the productive exchange while we read each other's manuscripts when simultaneously writing our books on Duchamp's readymade.

Last but not least thanks to the colleagues at the Hochschule für Grafik und Buchkunst for the sabbatical term in winter 2016 / 17.

Finally, the valuable support for this book from Séverine Gossart and Antoine Monnier representing the Association Marcel Duchamp should be given due credit.

CONTENT*

* part I and II may be read in any sequence, which may cause smaller repetitions

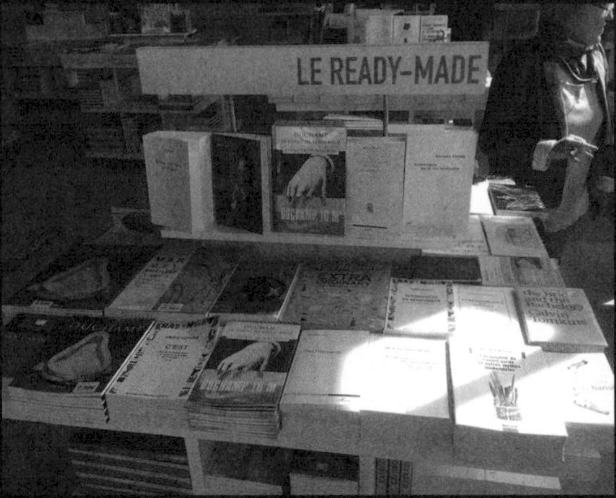

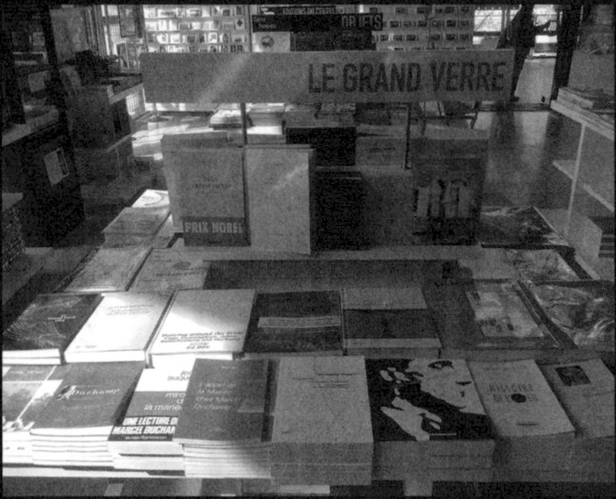

Display of books on the topics of the Readymade and the Large Glass *at the museum bookshop for the exhibition* Marcel Duchamp: La Peinture, même, *Centre Pompidou, Paris, September 24, 2014–January 5, 2015.*

I. READYMADE INDEX[1]

1 In the following, the spelling "ready-made" is used for the adjective outside of an art context, while "readymade" designates the "already made" works by Duchamp and other artists. Marcel Duchamp himself used various spellings in texts on his works and concepts. For a detailed analysis, see André Gervais, "Note sur le terme Readymade (ou ready-made)," in: *Étant donné Marcel Duchamp*, № 1, premier semestre, 1999, pp. 118–121.
Titles of works given by Marcel Duchamp are in italics with quotation marks (e.g. "*Pharmacy*" while descriptive designations are in italics only (e.g. *Bottle Dryer*).

What body of work do we talk about when we discuss "the readymades" of Marcel Duchamp?

While literature on the topic of the readymade has grown immensely, it still does not offer a direct answer to the simple question of to what extent and exact characteristics were Duchamp's activities. There is neither an established list of readymades, an agreed account of their genesis, nor a satisfyingly precise definition. Even the 2014–2017 centennial did not bring us an encyclopedia or a retrospective of the readymade.

This book will not overcome those deficits, nor could it hope to do so. Instead, my suggestion is to think about possible reasons for this vagueness of the readymade concept. Maybe there were structural motives in Duchamp's activities that continually prevent any fixed reading of this body of work?

As early as 1935, in one of the first art-theoretical texts on Duchamp ever, André Breton wrote with an eye on the artist of the readymades: "It will be of great interest to one day determine the full scope of his activities, each so radically unexpected, and in that sense to try and uncover the law of their development."[2]

This suggestion of a specifically inherent logic to the readymade's creation, which would define both its

2 André Breton, "Phare de la mariée," in: *Minotaure*, № 6, winter 1934 / 35, p. 46. ("Il sera de tout intérêt d'aborder un jour la portée de ses démarches, toujours rigoureusement inattendues, en ce sens, de tenter de dégager la loi de leur progression.")

extent and its delimitations, has hardly been followed at all. Instead, an irritating diversity of interpretations proliferates in the secondary literature, where the most various fields of knowledge are applied to the ready-made—non-Euclidean geometry, history of science, institutional theory of art, etc.

All of these interpretations share the assumption that we know what we talk about when we discuss "the readymades" of Marcel Duchamp. But that is not the case. Their plural masks ever new combinations that are often willfully adapted to the thesis at hand. The "full scope," as Breton saw it, or even the "law of their development," is not tackled in the attempts.

The mostly overlooked, very simple questions regarding the genesis, the extent, and the commonalities of "the readymades" will form the center of the next chapter. Our *Readymade Index* is not an inventory of readymades, and it does not aim to compensate for the lack of a catalogue raisonné. Instead, we will explore the conditions for the possibility (or impossibility) of such a catalog.[3] In contrast to the closed nature of a catalogue raisonné, an index can describe a fluid state, as demonstrated for example by the volatility of stock indexes.

3 Cf. the unfinished "catalogue raisonné of the readymades" undertaken between 1999 and 2006 in: *Étant donné Marcel Duchamp*, №1, 3, 5, 6, 7.

READYMADE CHRONOLOGY: WHEN DID THE "READYMADE CENTURY" BEGIN?

Can we define a certain moment that marks the inception of the readymade project? Can we perhaps denominate a prototypical "first readymade"? Various works and occasions from the period between 1913 and 1917 seem to offer themselves for the nomination:

Bicycle Wheel, Paris 1913: Against this, we can argue that the object was created and put together from two separate parts (wheel and stool), so in fact, it is a montage, and not an already made object chosen by the artist. Accordingly, it is not classified as a readymade by Duchamp in his *Boîte-en-valise*. In later interviews he always stressed that when he first mounted the *Bicycle Wheel* in his studio, it had no connection to the term readymade, which he would only hear later in the U.S.: "The word did not exist—the thought did not exist..."[4]

Bottle Dryer, Paris 1914: Here we have Duchamp's first unaltered object. He bought it in the Bazar de l'Hôtel de Ville department store in Paris with the idea of installing it in his studio. In 1914, it bore no signature and no title, and the term readymade had not yet been

4 Duchamp in a television interview from 1966; https://youtu.be/pHeNrmBPKKQ. Cf. similar statements by Duchamp in: Interview Charbonnier 1960–61, and interview Cabanne 1967, p. 51.

found. Both the *Bicycle Wheel* and the *Bottle Dryer* were left behind in Paris when Duchamp decided to center his life in New York in 1915 on account of the First World War. They were never exhibited and we do not know their exact appearance since the originals were never photographed.

"Pharmacie," Paris 1914: The first "already made" work signed and titled by Duchamp. However, he added two small paint blotches to this art print bought in a shop for art supplies, one in red and one in green. These blotches on the horizon of a winter landscape remind us of the lights of a pharmacy, which is where the work's title derives from. "*Pharmacie*" is an outlier among Duchamp's ready-made utility objects. The artist has appropriated the reproduction of an artwork and reinterpreted it as a new "original" through a minimal intervention in paint and a new title. He took "*Pharmacie*" with him when he moved to New York in 1915, where it entered the context of the American readymades (the other link was the *Bicycle Wheel* that he remade in New York in 1916). Thus "*Pharmacie*" is the only example from his time in Paris that still exists in its original form.

"In Advance of the Broken Arm," New York 1915: This snow shovel, the original of which has also been lost, is the first known object signed by Duchamp that bears a longer inscription in English. Forty-five years later, in his short lecture "Apropos of 'Readymades'," he reminisces: "In New York in 1915 I bought at a hardware store a snow shovel on which I wrote 'In advance of the broken arm.' It was around that time that the word 'Readymade' came to my mind to designate this form of manifestation."[5]

For the first time the linguistic dimension of the readymade comes to the fore. Duchamp has described his inscription as a "verbal color."[6] While he doesn't specify if the term readymade already played a part in his purchase of the shovel, at least the object and its designation came together "around that time." Duchamp's move from Paris to New York apparently was a decisive factor: only in the U.S. did he encounter the terminology of "ready-made," pre-produced commodities, objects off the shelf that are held in stock for prospective buyers so they don't have to be produced specifically on order or made to measure for the customer's wishes.

Duchamp's interest in the linguistic dimension was expressly connected to the term ready-made as such, when he came across it in the U.S.: "I was interested in the word," he would later say.[7]

5 Marcel Duchamp, "Apropos of 'Readymades,'" lecture at the symposium The Art of Assemblage, Museum of Modern Art, New York, October 19, 1961, first printed in: *Art and Artists*, London, vol. I, № 4, July 1966, p. 47.

6 Interview, Collin, 1967, p. 38. Cf. also related statements by Duchamp in: Interview, Charbonnier, 1960–61.

7 "Il m'a interessé comme mot." Interview Cabanne 1967, p. 51.

Letter from January 1916, in which Duchamp first uses the term readymade for his "all made" (*tout fait*) works of art: Following historiographical methods, the first written appearance of a name fixes its dating (in contrast to art-historical practice, which focuses on objects) and subsequent anniversaries e.g. of the founding of a city. The letter thus constitutes the first historical (but not necessarily the first art-historical) evidence for the concept of the readymade not tied to a single object.[8]

The letter is addressed to Duchamp's sister Suzanne and dated "around January 15." Duchamp's intention was to make the bottle dryer he bought in Paris two years earlier a "readymade at a distance."[9] He wanted to transfer the new term found in New York in 1915 / 16 to an object from 1914 left in Paris by way of the signature of his sister. This would have meant a threefold transfer: bestowing authorship on an object from 1914 retroactively in 1916, across the distance from New York to Paris, and through the agency of the artist's sister

8 Cf. Fabrice Lefaix, "Catalogue raisonné des ready-mades IV (In Advance of the Broken Arm)," in: *Étant donné Marcel Duchamp*, № 6, 2005, p. 220, note 2, which points to the fact that there are no indications for a use of the term before January 1916 in statements by either Duchamp or his contemporaries.

9 Francis M. Naumann and Hector Obalk (eds.), *Affect^{t} Marcel: The Selected Correspondence of Marcel Duchamp*, London 2000, p. 43f.

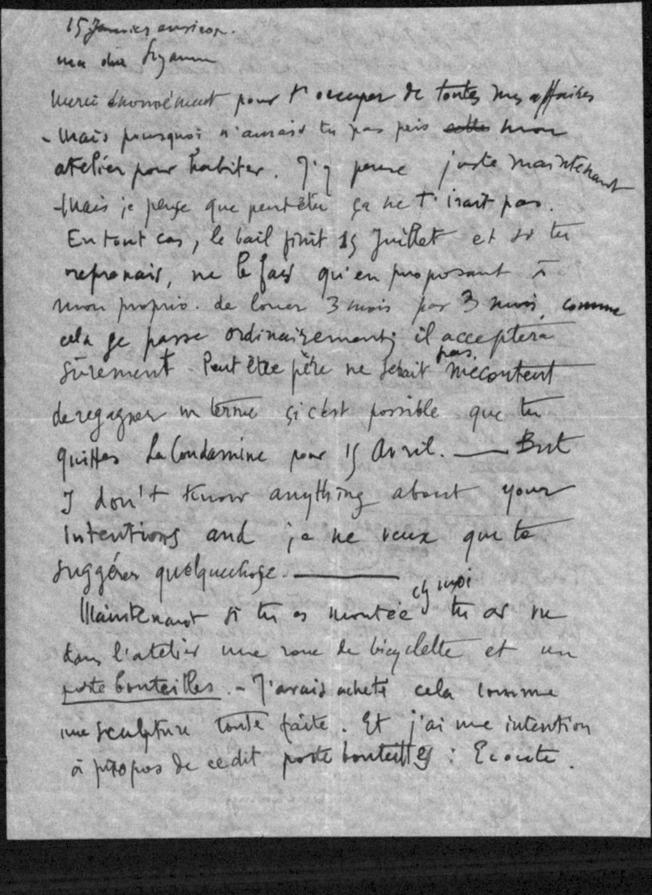

15 Janvier environ.
ma chère Suzanne
Merci énormément pour t'occuper de toutes mes affaires
- Mais pourquoi n'aurais tu pas pris ~~cet~~ mon atelier pour habiter. J'y pense juste maintenant
- Mais je pense que peut-être ça ne t'irait pas.
En tout cas, le bail finit 15 Juillet et si tu reprenais, ne le fais qu'en proposant à mon proprio. de louer 3 mois par 3 mois, comme cela se passe ordinairement; il acceptera sûrement. Peut-être père ne serait pas mécontent de regagner un terme si c'est possible que tu quittes La Condamine pour 15 Avril. —— But I don't know anything about your intentions and je ne veux que te suggérer quelquechose. ——
Maintenant si tu es montée chez moi tu as vu dans l'atelier une roue de bicyclette et un porte bouteilles. - J'avais acheté cela comme une sculpture toute faite. Et j'ai une intention à propos de ce dit porte bouteilles : Écoute.

Marcel Duchamp, letter to Suzanne Duchamp, January 15, [1916], Jean Crotti papers, Archives of American Art, Smithsonian Institution, Washington DC.

Ici, à N. Y., j'ai acheté des objets dans le même goût et je les traite comme des "readymade", tu sais assez d'anglais pour comprendre "le sens de "tout fait" que je donne à ces objets — Je les signe et je leur donne une inscription en anglais. Je te donne qques exemples:

J'ai par exemple une grande pelle à neige sur laquelle j'ai inscrit en bas: In advance of the broken arm. traduction française: En avance du bras cassé — Ne t'escrime pas trop à comprendre dans le sens romantique ou impressionniste ou cubiste — Cela n'a aucun rapport avec;

un autre "readymade" s'appelle: Emergency in favor of twice. traduction française possible: Danger ~~[illegible]~~ (crise) en faveur de 2 fois.

Tout ce préambule pour te dire:

Prends pour toi ce porte bouteilles. J'en fais un "Readymade" à distance. Tu inscriras en bas et à l'intérieur du cercle du bas en petites lettres peintes avec un pinceau à l'huile en couleur blanc d'argent la ~~plus~~ inscription que je vais te donner ci après, et tu signeras de la même écriture comme suit:

[d'après] Marcel Duchamp.

delegated to sign the object. This art-historically unique project failed due to a slow speed of transfer: the letter arrived after Duchamp's Paris studio had already been cleared.[10]

Exhibition in April 1916: In the catalog to the *Exhibition of Modern Art* at Bourgeois Galleries, New York, April 3rd to 29th, under the name "Duchamp, Marcel" in the "Sculptures" section, we find the following entry number 50: "Two Ready-mades." Here the term appears in print for the first time designating works of art instead of finished goods.

It is unknown which objects were on exhibition. Visitors as well as the press seem to have studiously avoided the two readymades, or maybe they simply didn't notice them. This becomes easier to understand when we bring to mind the context of the other sculptures displayed in the exhibition, such as the delicately elegant animal figures of Hunt Diederich, or a classically modernist *Seated Woman* by Raymond Duchamp-Villon.

Rejection of the urinal titled "Fountain" by the New York Society of Independent Artists in April 1917: There was no public reaction to any of the readymades before April 1917, as they were not exhibited by Duchamp again. Their presence in his studio was known only to a small circle of initiates, and the artist emphasized their pri-

10 On the issue of which inscription the *Bottle Dryer* was supposed to receive, see Lars Blunck, *Marcel Duchamp: Porte-bouteilles*, Nuremberg 2014, p. 83.

SCULPTURES

DIEDERICH, HUNT.

47. Greyhounds.
48. Dog and Antelope.
49. Hunter and Dogs.

DUCHAMP, MARCEL.

50. Two Ready-mades.

DUCHAMP-VILLON, RAYMOND.

51. Seated Woman.

Entry number 50: "Two Ready-mades," from the catalog to the Exhibition of Modern Art *at Bourgeois Galleries, New York, April 3 to 29, 1916.*

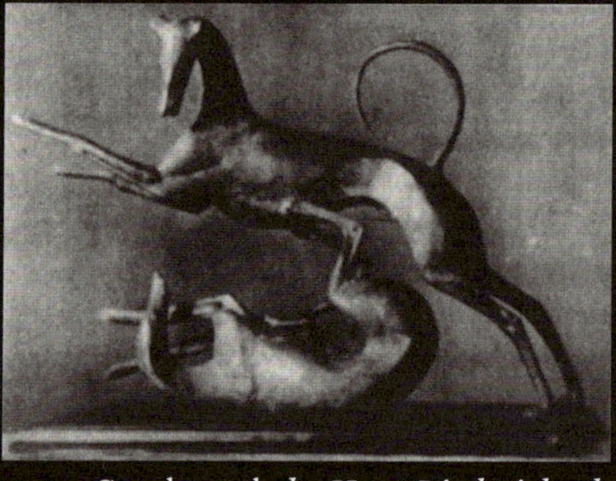

Greyhounds *by Hunt Diederich, shown at the* Exhibition of Modern Art *at Bourgeois Galleries, from: The New York Sun, April 4, 1916.*

vate character when he described them as "a little game between 'I' and 'me.'"[11]

The submission and subsequent rejection of "Fountain" provoked the first and only public controversy during the founding era of the readymade. Most contemporaries did not learn who was behind the signature "R. Mutt" on the urinal. The collector and art patron Katherine Dreier, for example, who was close to Duchamp for decades, was on the board of the Independents and voted against including "Fountain" in the exhibition. In the meager public response to the incident, the term readymade was not used. Most of the debate focused on the propriety of showing a urinal in a jury-free art exhibition, not on a work or concept by Marcel Duchamp.

This is verified by a letter from Katherine Dreier. Three weeks after the incident she suggested to William Glackens—the president of the Independents—"that we invite Marcel Duchamp to lecture one afternoon in our free lecture hall on his 'Readymades' and have Richard Mutt bring the discarded object and explain the theory of art and why it had a legitimate place in an Art Exhibit."[12]

11 Calvin Tomkins, *Duchamp: A Biography*, New York 1996, p. 160. Cf. Dieter Daniels, *Duchamp und die anderen – Der Modellfall einer künstlerischen Wirkungsgeschichte in der Moderne*, Cologne 1992, pp. 214–217.

12 Letter by Katherine Dreier from April 26, 1917. In: William A. Camfield, *Marcel Duchamp: Fountain*, Houston 1989, p. 31.

At the time, Duchamp did his best to cover up his role in the "Richard Mutt Case."[13] He did it so successfully that we still cannot fully clarify who actually submitted the urinal and in what regard we can describe Duchamp as the author of this most famous of all readymades (which will be discussed later). Still, the incident of April 1917 marks the historical beginning for the readymade having any sort of public reception, whose consequences can still be felt today.

SUMMARY: There was no first Readymade

So apparently there is no single first decisive moment of the readymade, no flash of inspiration that found immediate realization, instead we have a series of indi-

13 This can be seen in the magazine *The Blind Man*, published one month later, which covers the "Richard Mutt Case" in some detail, but without any reference to Duchamp. Duchamp is mentioned only once in the issue, as the creator of "*Broyeuse de Chocolat Nº 2*," pictured on the cover. The term readymade is not used. (*The Blind Man*, P.T.B., Nº 2, May 1917. The editor of this magazine was Beatrice Wood, in collaboration with Henri-Pierre Roché and Marcel Duchamp, both uncredited).

Fountain by R. Mutt

Photograph by Alfred Stieglitz

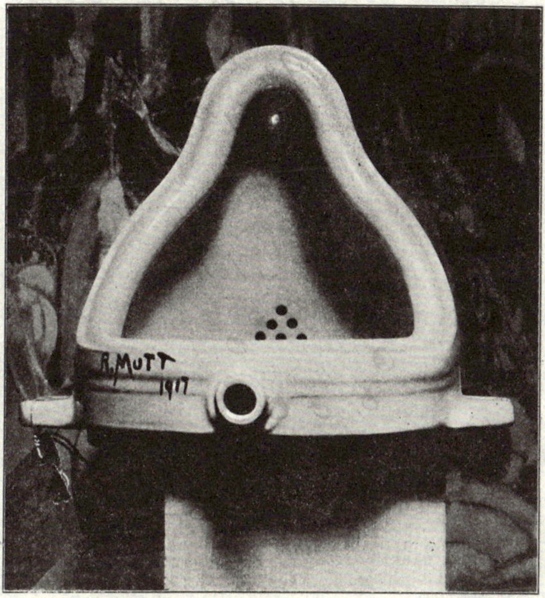

THE EXHIBIT REFUSED BY THE INDEPENDENTS

Page from The Blind Man, P.T.B., *№ 2, May 1917, with Alfred Stieglitz's photo of the original* "Fountain." *The identities of R. Mutt or Marcel Duchamp are not revealed in the magazine.*

cators for a gradual genesis. First we should note that the objects existed in Paris *before* the concept of the readymade was formed. "The thing," Duchamp himself said, "arrived before the idea."[14] So we have to let go of the thought that Duchamp would have developed a concept and terminology of the readymade and then proceeded to find some fitting object. The objects and their designation seem to have connected more slowly, they intermingled with time.

Thus in a readymade the creative process shifts from the manual fabrication of an artwork to a thoughtful reflection on something that has already been made. A note by Duchamp from 1913 already indicates the full depth of his enquiry: "Can one make works which are not works of 'art'?"[15] Four years later this programmatic note is fulfilled, when the urinal is rejected by an art exhibition that due to its motto, "No jury, no prizes," should not reject any kind of work at all.

Initially the creation of the readymades stopped after 1918, not least since Duchamp left New York in August 1918, after the U.S. had entered the First World War, and moved to Buenos Aires for ten months. Before leaving, he arranged some of the readymades in his studio and photographed their shadows. This resulting

14 Duchamp referring to the Bicycle Wheel: "La chose – la roue de bicyclette – est venue avant l'idée." Interview Hahn, 1966 b, p. 61.

15 Michel Sanouillet and Elmer Peterson, *The Essential Writings of Marcel Duchamp (Salt Seller)*, London 1978, p. 74.

"Can one make works which are not works of 'art'?" work note by Marcel Duchamp 1913 published in "À L'Infinitif" (The White Box), *1966.*

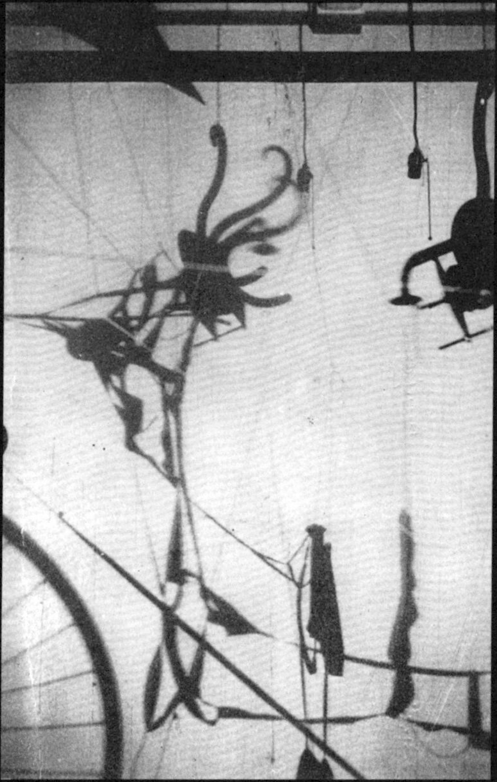

Marcel Duchamp, "Ombres portées," *1918, shadows of the Readymades* Hat-Rack, Bicycle Wheel, "In Advance of the Broken Arm" *(top left, truncated) and* "À Bruit secret," *arranged in a constellation around* Sculpture de Voyage. *In the top right, overlapping with* "À Bruit secret," *another, as yet unidentified object can be discerned.*

photographic work, titled "*Ombres portées*," can be understood as a last collective view from a selection of chosen objects that would remain in New York and have almost been completely lost afterward.

In summary, we can use the evidence presented here to specify that the core phase for "ready-made" objects in the U.S. lay in the one and a half years between January 1916 (first mention of the term in a letter) and April 1917 (rejection of "*Fountain*").

As we have come to expect from Duchamp, there are exceptions to the rule. For example, in 1918, while he worked as secretary to an envoy of the French army in New York, he crossed out his own typewriting on a sheet of notepaper and then signed it. We can see this work both as a two-dimensional readymade and as a goodbye to the restrictions of the First World War, which he escaped with his departure for Buenos Aires.[16]

From his time in Buenos Aires we only know of the "*Readymade malheureux*" of 1919, for which he again sent instructions to his sister, similar to those for the *Bottle Dryer*. This time, though, Suzanne also had to purchase the object: a geometry book, to be left to the wind and weather, slowly falling to pieces.

16 Arturo Schwarz, *The Complete Works of Marcel Duchamp*, New York 2000, work № 352, identified as *French Military Paper*, with its "present location unknown."

Maybe a Last Readymade?

Dating the end of Duchamp's readymade activities becomes just as difficult as their beginnings. We know that after a series of transformations and variations he abandoned them in the mid 1920s—only to continue again in the 1940s, among others with objects that accompanied the luxury editions of *Boîte-en-valise* (*Padlock*, 1948) and the monograph *Sur Marcel Duchamp* by Robert Lebel ("*Eau & gaz à tous les étages*," 1958).

With a certain regularity, Duchamp created more readymades until his last years, always following the principle of a limited number. Examples include: *Three Mirrors*, 1964 (signed in the silver layer on the back), "*rasée L.H.O.O.Q.*," 1965 (invitation to an exhibition preview, inscribed by hand and signed in an edition of ca. 100 copies), "*Hommage à Caissa*," 1966 (signed chessboard, planned edition of 30 pieces, though in the end only around ten were produced), "*Pollyperruque*," 1967 (greeting card in Spanish with dedication). Just like the readymades created between 1914 and 1917, these later works cannot be unambiguously categorized, indeed they contribute to a certain blurring at the fringes of the readymade concept.[17]

17 André Gervais' chronological list of 56 entries covers the period from 1913 to 1967, which he separates into two segments, 1913 to 1927 and 1943 to 1967; André Gervais, "Liste des Readymades de Marcel Duchamp (1913–1967)," in:

READYMADE NOMENCLATURE: WHICH WORKS OF DUCHAMP DOES HE DESCRIBE AS READYMADES?

A) IN THE BOÎTE-EN-VALISE

If Duchamp's readymade activities cannot be dated with certainty, what about their extent? Is there a clearly defined corpus of readymades within the artist's oeuvre? Duchamp characterized himself as a very meticulous person, so we might first want to take recourse to *Boîte-en-valise*, the painstakingly edited documentation of his own work. We will leave out the variations and derivatives of the readymade introduced by Duchamp himself, since the situation appears muddled enough as it is.

Boîte-en-valise was compiled by Duchamp between 1936 and 1941 and it contains eight works labeled as a "readymade"—solely as a readymade, without additional modifiers like the *readymade rectifié* (rectified readymade) or *readymade aidé* (assisted readymade). Of these eight works, only three are still extant in their original form; the others we know merely through photographs and / or later replicas:

- "*Pharmacie,*" 1914 (original in private collection)
- *Bottle Dryer*, 1914 (original lost)

Étant donne Marcel Duchamp, № 1, premier semestre, 1999, pp. 122–125. Thomas Zaunschirm dedicated a whole book to Duchamp's supposed "last readymade" from 1963 (Thomas Zaunschirm, Faux Vagin: *Marcel Duchamp's Last Readymade*, Ostfildern 2015).

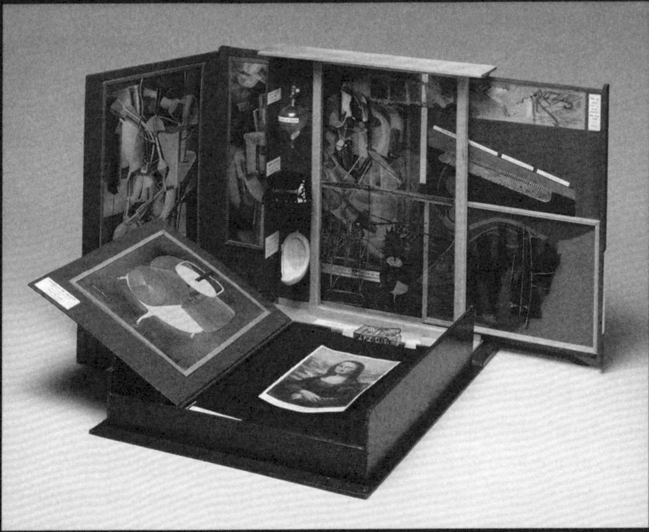

Marcel Duchamp, Boîte-en-valise, *1936–1941 (Edition G).*

With his Boîte-en-valise, *Duchamp provides the first comprehensive representation of the readymades, including titles and dates for the individual pieces that are still accepted today.*

- *"In Advance of the Broken Arm,"* 1915 (original lost)
- *Comb*, 1916 (original in the Philadelphia Museum of Art)
- *"... Pliant ... de voyage,"* 1916 (original lost)
- *"Fountain,"* 1917 (original lost)
- *Hat Rack*, 1917 (original lost)
- *"Air de Paris,"* 1919 (broken but later the original was restored at the Philadelphia Museum of Art)

More than 20 years into their history, Duchamp's own compilation offers a first overview of the readymades as a work group, which helps us define what Breton called the "scope of his activities, each so radically unexpected." The artist did not count the *Bicycle Wheel* among the readymades, while "*Pharmacie*" and the *Bottle Dryer* from his days in Paris were declared readymades after the fact. Especially the latter case appears legitimate because of the artist's letter to Suzanne Duchamp from January 1916.

A piece that appears to be missing is the coat hanger titled "*Trébuchet*" (Trap), once fixed to the floor of the artist's studio, "33 West 67th. New-York," beside the *Bicycle Wheel*. It is described in *Boîte-en-valise* as "porte-manteau, accroché au sol," which imparts it with a mainly situative meaning, whereas the other readymades are introduced as solitary objects.

Duchamp developed a whole palette of strategies for representing the readymades in *Boîte-en-valise*. This was partly influenced by their very diverse states of recorded documentation. At the same time, Duchamp made evaluations and interpretations. He staged the readymades within *Boîte-en-valise* not as a homogenous work group but as a sequence of individual pieces.

Boîte-en-valise: Printed representations of Readymades:

- "*Pharmacie,*" 1914: full color reproduction of the original
- *Bottle Dryer*, 1914: five layer print after black and white photograph (by Man Ray) of a later replica (from 1936), labeled "Ready made" (no title) dated 1914 (no reference to the replica)
- "*In Advance of the Broken Arm,*" 1915: reworked and colorized historical photograph of the lost original
- *Comb*, 1916: full color reproduction of the original, labeled "Ready made" (no title)
- *Hat Rack*, 1917: reworked and colorized historical photograph of the lost original, labeled "Ready made" (no title)

Boîte-en-valise: Miniature models in the material of the originals:

- "... *Pliant* ... *de voyage,*" 1916: wax cloth, without historical reference
- "*Fountain,*" 1917: porcelain model after historical photograph of the lost original
- "*Air de Paris,*" 1919: glass model after the original

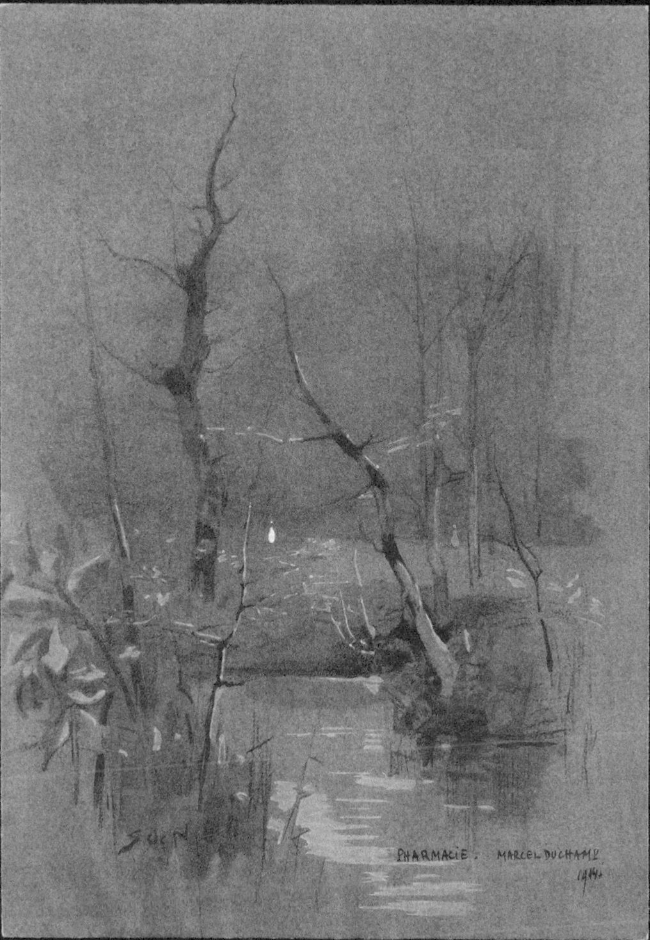

Pharmacie

(Ready made; haut. $0^{m}25$)

Rouen, Jan. 1914

Coll. Man Ray

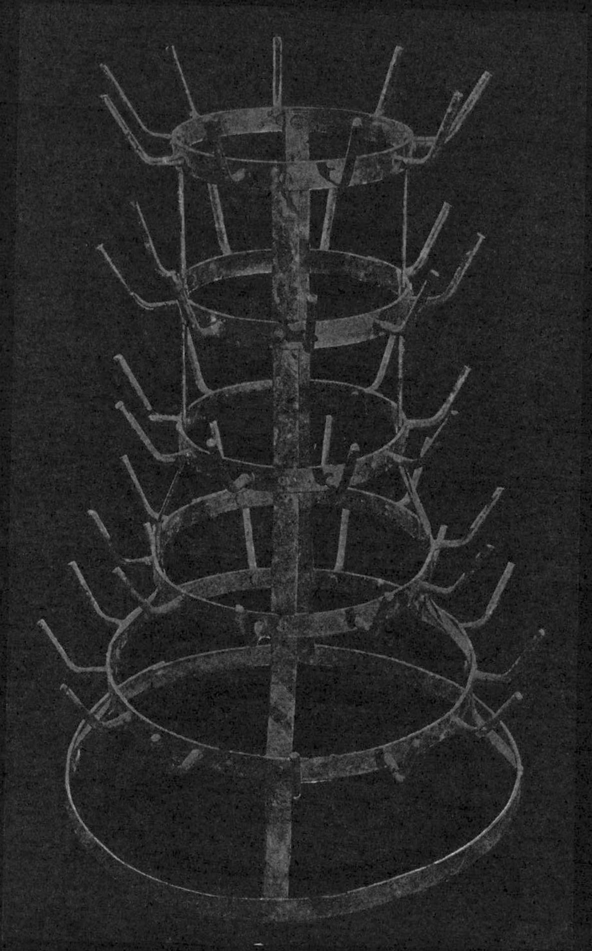

Ready made

(Fer galvanisé;
haut. $0^{m}59$, diam. base $0^{m}37$)

Paris 1914

Coll. Man Ray

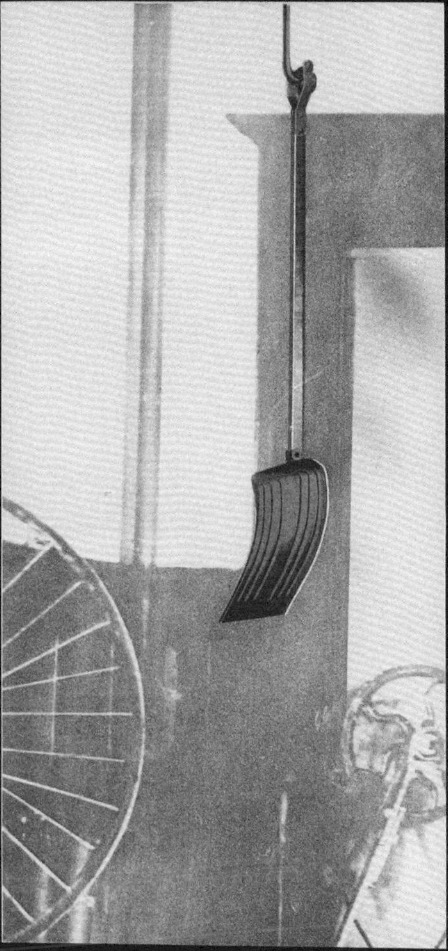

In advance of the broken arm

(Ready made; haut. 1 m)

New-York, 1915

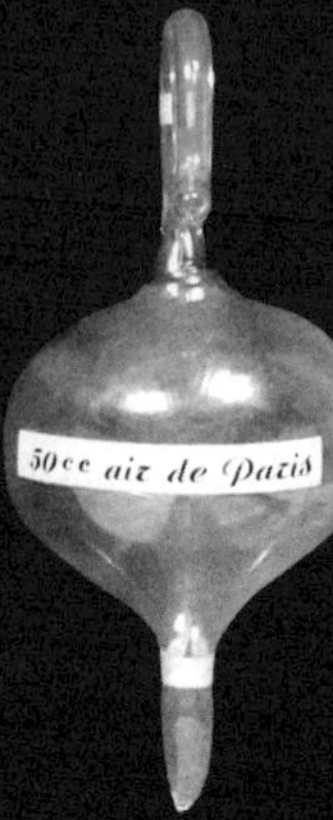

50cc air de Paris
(Ready made; haut. 0m12)
Paris, 1919
Coll. Arensberg

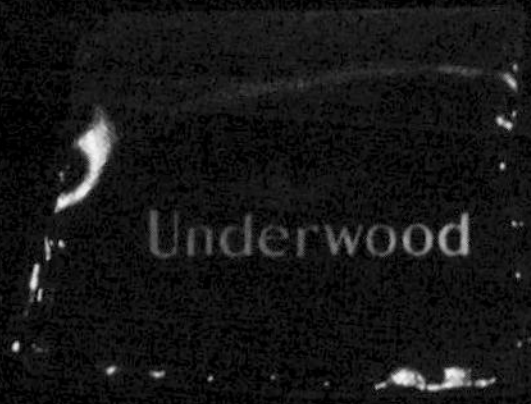

... pliant, ...de voyage.
(Ready made; haut. 0m23)
New-York, 1917

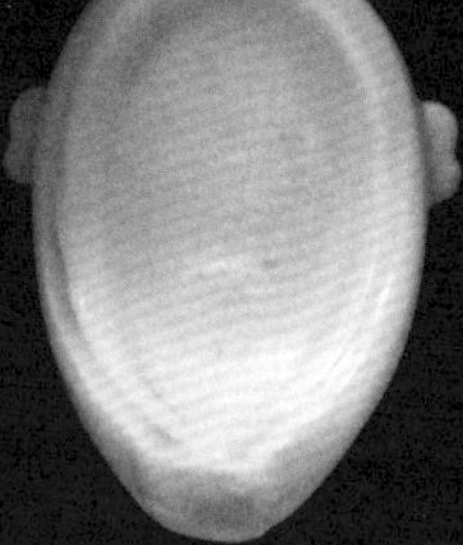

Fountain
by Richard MUTT
(Ready made; haut. 0m60)
New-York, 1917

Marcel Duchamp, Comb, *three versions:*

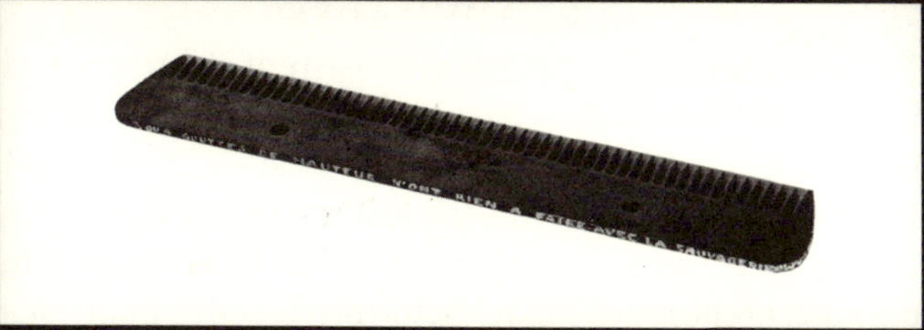

Comb, *1916, original, Philadelphia Museum of Art*

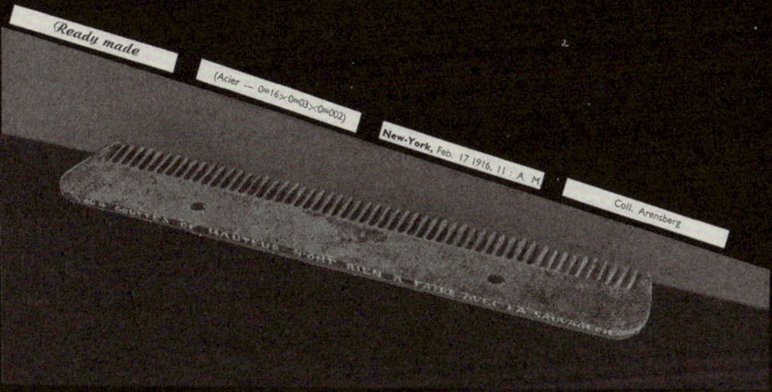

Comb, *representation in* Boîte-en-valise

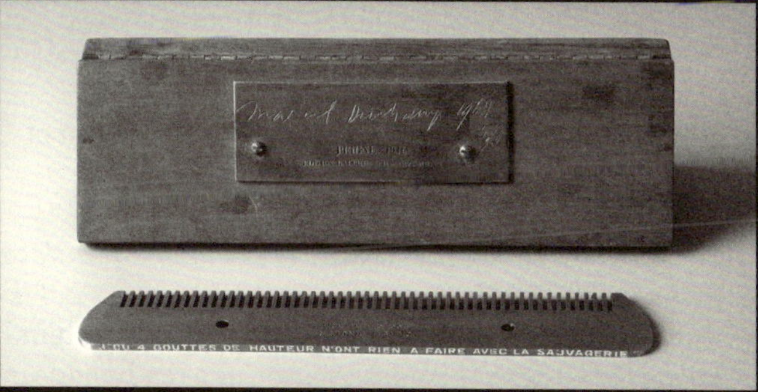

Comb, *Multiple Edition Schwarz 1964*

B) IN THE MULTIPLE EDITION OF '14 READYMADES'

Two decades later, a much less consistent view is offered by an edition of "14 Readymades," authorized by Duchamp and published as multiples in eight identical, handmade copies of the mostly lost original readymades by Galleria Arturo Schwarz in 1964. Aside from the paradox of the readymades being produced as multiples (more about that later), the spectrum of objects defined as readymades has become much larger. In addition to the readymades from *Boîte-en-valise* there are seven more works (five of which still exist as an original):

- *Bicycle Wheel*, 1913 / 16 (original lost)
- "*3 Stoppages Étalon,*" 1913 / 14 (original in the Museum of Modern Art, New York)
- "*À Bruit secret,*" 1916 (original in the Philadelphia Museum of Art, described in *Boîte-en-valise* as a readymade aidé)
- "*Apolinère Enameled,*" 1916 / 17 (original in the Philadelphia Museum of Art, described in *Boîte-en-valise* as a readymade rectifié)
- "*Trébuchet,*" 1917 (original lost)
- "*Why Not Sneeze, Rose Sélavy?,*" 1921 (original in the Philadelphia Museum of Art)
- "*Fresh Widow,*" 1920 (original in the Museum of Modern Art, New York)

Of these seven, two are described as a *readymade aidé* or a *readymade rectifié* respectively in Duchamp's *Boîte-en-valise*, but none as a pure readymade. On the other hand, "*Pharmacie*"—despite its designation as a readymade in *Boîte-en-valise*—is missing in the edition of multiples

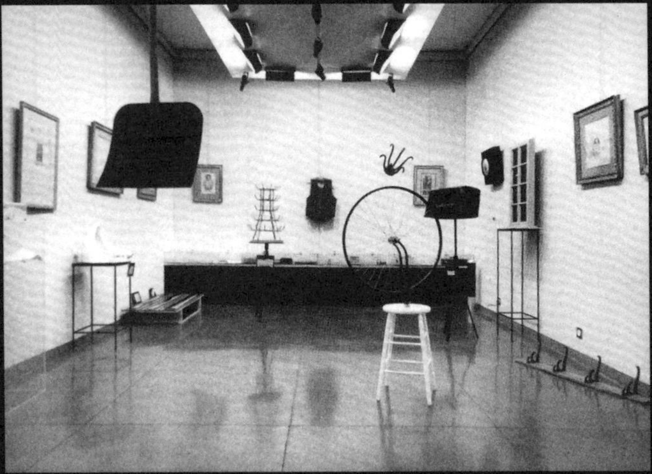

Presentation of the Readymades at Omaggio a Marcel Duchamp, *Galleria Schwarz, Milan, June 5 to September 30, 1964 (photograph by Ugo Mulas). As several multiples where still in production, Arturo Schwarz borrowed replicas by Ulf Linde from the Moderna Museet Stockholm for the exhibition.* *(see also p. 129 in this book for details)*

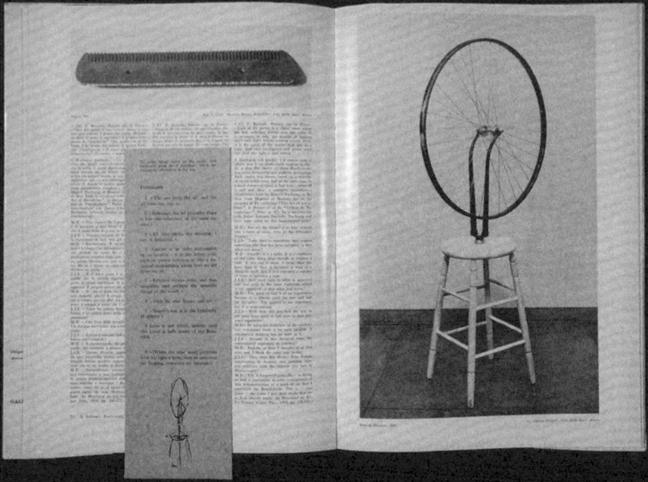

Double page from: Walter Hopps; Ulf Linde; Arturo Schwarz; Marcel Duchamp: Ready-mades, etc. (1913–1964), *Galleria Schwarz, Milan and Le Terrain Vague, Paris 1964.*

Left: Comb, *replica by Ulf Linde, right:* Bicycle Wheel, *multiple by Galleria Schwarz.*

In the trilingual publication accompanying the exhibition, which was co-designed by Duchamp himself, most illustrations do not show the 1964 multiples by Galleria Schwarz, but instead the replicas created by Ulf Linde in 1963, because the production of the ready-mades was not finished on schedule.

from 1964, probably because it had previously been produced in an edition of 100 in 1945 to accompany an issue of *View Magazine*. Also missing is the bearded Mona Lisa, "L.H.O.O.Q." from 1919, which in *Boîte-en-valise* had been included as a *readymade rectifié*.[18]

By excluding these two-dimensional works, the edition of multiples distorts the overall impression made by this body of work and pushes it toward object art, positioning the readymades as a precursor of this defining art genre of the 1960s.

While this line of argument may appear somewhat pedantic, it consequently leads us to a more rousing appeal: the prevalent canonization of the edition "14 Readymades" by museums and publications worldwide must be revised! This edition manufactures the illusion of a well-defined work group, but its compilation follows no inner logic. The subtle differences in the representation of each readymade that we find in *Boîte-en-valise* is smoothened out by a replication of the objects in their original size. The lack of consistency in their combination is merely hidden behind the superficial conformity of these 'actual size' exhibits.[19] Despite all of this, these

18 A separate edition of "*L.H.O.O.Q.*" would later be published by Galleria Schwarz in 1965, in an edition of 38 copies as a special supplement to a book by Pierre de Massot.

19 There are also many contradictions between the edition of multiples and the catalog of works edited by Arturo Schwarz just five years later (*The Complete Works*

14 objects still determine the way readymades are represented in exhibitions and reproductions to this day.

Such a classic museum presentation of the objects also leads to a neglect of their situational aspects, which for example appear in the coat hanger fixed to the floor of the artist's New York studio, or in contemporary photographs of the different modes of presentation for the urinal (hanging from the doorframe in the studio, lying on a pedestal, etc.)[20]

of Marcel Duchamp, London 1969). For example, Schwarz categorizes "*3 Stoppages Étalon*" as an assemblage, and not as a readymade, while "*Fresh Widow*" is described as a "miniature French window"—despite the fact that as multiples they both belong among the "14 Readymades." It also remains elusive why "*La Bagarre d'Austerlitz*" from 1921 is not part of the edition of multiples, while "*Fresh Widow*" is. In *Boîte-en-valise* they are both labeled simply as "window" (*fenêtre*). Probably this was mainly due to commercial interests (like in the case of the ommission of "*Pharmacie*" because of the View edition): "*La Bagarre d'Austerlitz*" had already been published in a miniature edition that came with André Breton's *Au lavoir noir (avec une fenêtre de Marcel Duchamp)*, Editions G.L.M., Paris 1936. (Thanks to Herbert Molderings who pointed out the 1936 edition)

As was to be expected from Duchamp, there again is an exception to the rule established by the edition of readymades as multiples from 1964. In the same year, also through Galleria Schwarz, the artist published the etching "*Pulled at Four Pins*," a delicate line drawing of a chimney ventilator, supposedly the rendering of an eponymous readymade created shortly after Duchamp's arrival in the U.S. This work challenges the canonical claims of the "14 Readymades": "*Pulled at Four Pins*" quietly points to the fact that their compilation cannot be thought to be comprehensive—as an addendum to the edition of multiples it explodes their seeming finality.[21]

20 Cf. Elena Filipovic, *A Museum That Is Not*, 2009, online at https://e-flux.com/journal/a-museum-that-is-not.

21 Since "*Pulled at Four Pins*" is also missing from *Boîte-en-valise*, this selection of readymades likewise appears incomplete in retrospect. The chimney ventilator is mentioned as a readymade in texts by André Breton (1935) and Gabriièle Buffet-Picabia (1936) even before *Boîte-en-valise*. See Schwarz, *Complete Works*, № 372 and 609.

READYMADE COMMENTARY: WHAT DOES DUCHAMP SAY ABOUT THE READYMADES?

After we've failed to discern any consistency in the "14 Readymades" from 1964 (and we shouldn't underestimate Arturo Schwarz's contributions to the confusion), let us next try to find more clarity in Duchamp's own words. Indeed the artist has dedicated one of the few texts in which he speaks about his work to the readymades. At a symposium held in conjunction with the 1961 exhibition *The Art of Assemblage* at the Museum of Modern Art in New York, which was met with much controversy at the time, he gave the lecture "Apropos of Readymades," surviving till this day as a typescript. In this brief text, Duchamp names only three examples for the genesis of the concept *(Bicycle Wheel*, 1913, "*Pharmacy*," 1914, and the *Snow Shovel*, 1915). He does not comment on the extent of his project.

He does however stress the importance of keeping the number of readymades limited: "I realized very soon the danger of repeating indiscriminately this form of expression and decided to limit the production of 'Readymades' to a small number yearly. I was aware at that time, that for the spectator even more than for the artist, art is a habit forming drug and I wanted to protect my 'Readymades' against such contamination."[22]

His second main concern, which he also emphasizes in many later statements, is aesthetic indifference:

22 Marcel Duchamp, "Apropos of ready-mades," (see p. 46 in this book) 1961

"This choice was based on a reaction of visual indifference with at the same time a total absence of good or bad taste... in fact a complete anesthesia."[23] Other speakers at the symposium included Richard Huelsenbeck and Robert Rauschenberg; Duchamp's remarks can be understood as an attempt to disassociate his work from Dadaism and Pop art.

In countless interviews after 1964, Duchamp was questioned on the readymades—not least because the edition of multiples meant they were suddenly present at exhibitions. Most questions were pointed toward the time of the readymades' origins in the years between 1914 and 1917. The multiples from 1964 were only rarely addressed explicitly, despite the fact that they gave the actual occasion for these interviews. The rather confusing selection of the "14 Readymades" was ignored completely.

At the same time, Duchamp delivered substantial statements on the conceptual background of the readymades apropos of these multiples, statements which still serve as the basis of most theoretical approaches to the readymade today.[24] All in all, the artist offered a relatively consistent commentary in interviews—we might also say: he offered a new conceptual framework for

23 Ibid.

24 Both in conversation and in correspondence, Marcel Duchamp confined himself to answering the questions put to him. Apart from five short lectures for specific occasions, there are no autonomous art-theoretical texts by Duchamp.

APROPOS OF 'READYMADES'

IN 1913 I HAD THE HAPPY IDEA TO FASTEN A BICYCLE WHEEL TO A KITCHEN STOOL AND WATCH IT TURN.

A FEW MONTHS LATER I BOUGHT A CHEAP REPRODUCTION OF A WINTER EVENING LANDSCAPE, WHICH I CALLED 'PHARMACY' AFTER ADDING TWO SMALL DOTS, ONE RED AND ONE YELLOW, IN THE HORIZON.

IN NEW YORK IN 1915 I BOUGHT AT A HARDWARE STORE A SNOW SHOVEL ON WHICH I WROTE 'IN ADVANCE OF THE BROKEN ARM'.

IT WAS AROUND THAT TIME THAT THE WORD 'READYMADE' CAME TO MIND TO DESIGNATE THIS FORM OF MANIFESTATION.

A POINT WHICH I WANT VERY MUCH TO ESTABLISH IS THAT THE CHOICE OF THESE 'READYMADES' WAS NEVER DICTATED BY AN ESTHETIC DELECTATION.

THIS CHOICE WAS BASED ON A REACTION OF VISUAL INDIFFERENCE WITH AT THE SAME TIME A TOTAL ABSENCE OF GOOD OR BAD TASTE . . . IN FACT A COMPLETE ANESTHESIA.

ONE IMPORTANT CHARACTERISTIC WAS THE SHORT SENTENCE WHICH I OCCASIONALLY INSCRIBED ON THE 'READYMADE'.

THAT SENTENCE INSTEAD OF DESCRIBING THE OBJECT LIKE A TITLE WAS MEANT TO CARRY THE MIND OF THE SPECTATOR TOWARDS OTHER REGIONS MORE VERBAL.

SOMETIMES I WOULD ADD A GRAPHIC DETAIL OF PRESENTATION WHICH IN ORDER TO SATISFY MY CRAVING FOR ALLITERATIONS, WOULD BE CALLED 'READYMADE AIDED'.

AT ANOTHER TIME WANTING TO EXPOSE THE BASIC ANTINOMY BETWEEN ART AND READYMADES I IMAGINED A 'RECIPROCAL READYMADE': USE A REMBRANDT AS AN IRONING BOARD!

I REALIZED VERY SOON THE DANGER OF REPEATING INDISCRIMINATELY THIS FORM OF EXPRESSION AND DECIDED TO LIMIT THE PRODUCTION OF 'READYMADES' TO A SMALL NUMBER YEARLY. I WAS AWARE AT THAT TIME, THAT FOR THE SPECTATOR EVEN MORE THAN FOR THE ARTIST, ART IS A HABIT FORMING DRUG AND I WANTED TO PROTECT MY 'READYMADES' AGAINST SUCH CONTAMINATION.

ANOTHER ASPECT OF THE 'READYMADE' IS ITS LACK OF UNIQUENESS . . . THE REPLICA OF A 'READYMADE' DELIVERING THE SAME MESSAGE; IN FACT NEARLY EVERY ONE OF THE 'READYMADES' EXISTING TODAY IS NOT AN ORIGINAL IN THE CONVENTIONAL SENSE.

A FINAL REMARK TO THIS EGOMANIAC'S DISCOURSE:

SINCE THE TUBES OF PAINT USED BY THE ARTIST ARE MANUFACTURED AND READY MADE PRODUCTS WE MUST CONCLUDE THAT ALL THE PAINTINGS IN THE WORLD ARE 'READYMADES AIDED' AND ALSO WORKS OF ASSEMBLAGE.

Marcel Duchamp 1961

Marcel Duchamp, "Apropos of Readymades," *magazine facsimile of the talk at* The Art of Assemblage, *Museum of Modern Art, New York, October 19, 1961. First published in* Art and Artists, *vol. I, № 4 (July 1966), p. 47.*

works which at that point already lay half a century in the past.

Interestingly, in several interviews Duchamp points to the fact that the readymades were not publicly presented at the time of their creation. He is recorded by a reporter of the *Minnesota Daily* as saying: "Actually they were a very personal experiment that I had never expected to show to the public. But I'm very pleased by the response to them."[25] The artist's extensive retrospective comments on the occasion of the "14 Readymades," which were shown in a large number of international exhibitions, implicitly raise the question what changes this "personal experiment" underwent in its subsequent musealization and canonization.

Already at the time of their original creation, Duchamp saw the importance of limiting the number of readymades, as documented in a note from the *Green Box*: "Limit the no. of rdymades yearly (?)."[26] Furthermore, Gabrièle Buffet-Picabia, in one of the earliest art-theoretical texts on the readymades, wrote: "His choice is the result of a strict elimination."[27] So let us go back to

25 Anon., "Artist Marcel Duchamp visits U-classes, exhibits at Walker," *Minnesota Daily*, October 22, 1965.

26 Michel Sanouillet and Elmer Peterson (eds.), *The Writings of Marcel Duchamp*, New York: Da Capo, 1989, p. 33.

27 Gabrièle Buffet, "Cœurs volants," in: *Cahiers d'Art*, nos. 1–2, 1936, p. 39. French: "...car sons choix participe

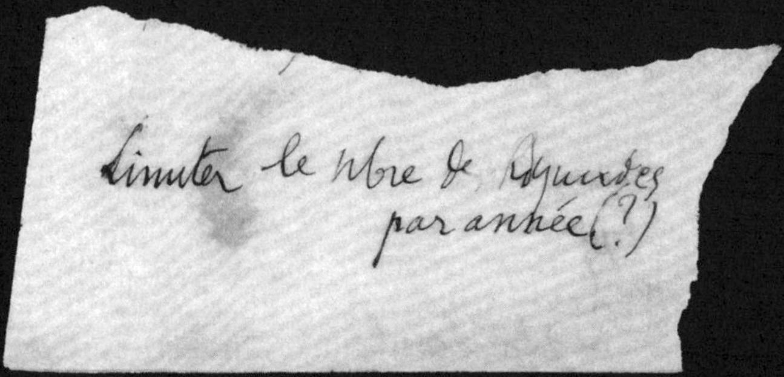

Note by Marcel Duchamp "Limit the no. of rdymades yearly (?)."
(Photo of the original note in the collection of the Centre Pompidou, Paris also included in the Green Box*)*

Breton's question, so far unanswered, as to the "scope" of these activities.

If limiting the number of readymades was so important to Duchamp, the question of how many readymades actually were legitimized by the artist imposes itself all the more. Neither our Readymade Chronology nor the Readymade Nomenclature have provided a definite number. And it is exactly here that the usually concise commentary by the artist lets us down.

There are two videos in which Duchamp rather casually mentions a total number of 13 readymades. In a 1965 discussion with Martin Friedman in front of an audience at the Walker Art Center he says: "In fact I only made thirteen of them in my life, in forty years, so it's not very much of an occupation."[28] Likewise, in a television interview with Joan Bakewell of the BBC in 1968 he mentions "the thirteen readymades I made in the course of thirty years."[29] Thirteen is one less than the number of the "14 Readymades" in the edition of multiples from 1964, which needs to be revised anyway.[30]

lui-même d'une stricte élimination." The illustrations to the text show Man Ray's photograph of a later *Bottle Dryer* from 1936, captioned as "Ready-made 1914," and "*Why Not Sneeze, Rose Sélavy?*," captioned as "Ready-made aidé, 1921."

28 Interview Friedman, 1965.

29 Interview Bakewell, 1968, p. 304.

30 The multiple edition from 1964 at first was only 13 Readymades, "*Apolinère Enameled*" was only added in 1965 (see-

But it remains a mystery why Duchamp speaks of a period of thirty or forty years respectively.

Especially confusing is a conversation with Otto Hahn from 1966, first published in an English translation, then (posthumously) in 1970 in the original French. In English, Duchamp speaks of "the ten or twelve readymades." In contrast to that, in French he mentions "the 30 or 35 readymades."[31] Why has the number suddenly almost tripled? Possibly Duchamp's statement has been redacted or falsified—in the English or in the French version? Unfortunately we do not know.[32] Even more confusing are the two lists of readymades reproduced on the following pages.

Schwarz, *Complete Works*, № 344).

31 Interview Hahn 1966a / 1966b. See for details the always meticulous German collection by Serge Stauffer, *Marcel Duchamp: Interviews und Statements*, Ostfildern 1992, p. 207.

32 This number would correspond to André Gervais' list of 35 realized or planned readymades (inclusive of all derivates) for the period from 1913 to 1927; André Gervais, *La Raie alitée d'effets*, Ville La Salle (Quebec) 1984, p. 83; cf. also Schwarz, *Complete Works*, p. 46. It is improbable that this higher number includes the late readymades after 1950, as those are not mentioned in the interview.

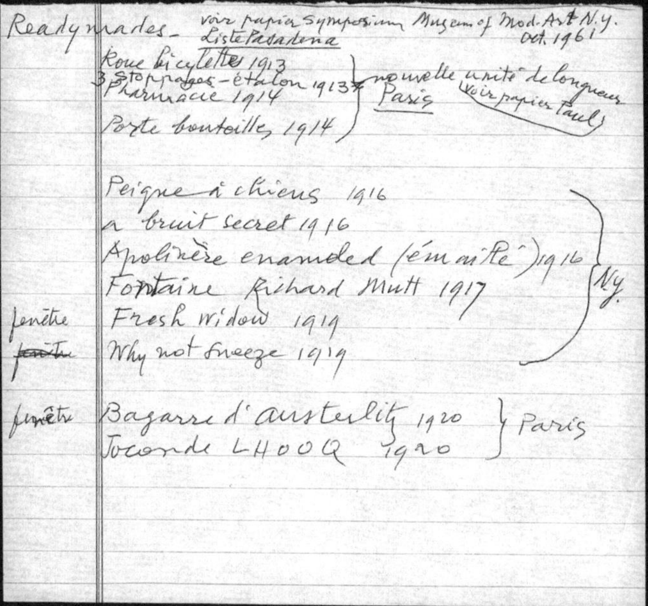

Readymades – voir papier Symposium Museum of Mod. Art N.Y. Oct. 1961
Liste Pasadena

Roue bicyclette 1913
3 Stoppages-étalon 1913–14
Pharmacie 1914
Porte bouteilles 1914
} nouvelle unité de longueur (voir papier Paul)
Paris

Peigne à chiens 1916
à bruit secret 1916
Apolinère enameled (émaillé) 1916
Fontaine Richard Mutt 1917
fenêtre Fresh widow 1919
~~fenêtre~~ Why not sneeze 1919
} N.Y.

fenêtre Bagarre d'Austerlitz 1920
Joconde LHOOQ 1920
} Paris

Marcel Duchamp, previously unpublished note, list of readymades, not dated. Philadelphia Museum of Art, Library and Archives. Alexina and Marcel Duchamp Papers, Lectures 1949–1964.

The list has three groups of readymades according to the location of there creation: Paris (1913–1914) / New York (1916–1920) / Paris (1920).

On the top of the page Marcel Duchamp's A propos of Readymades *talk (October 19, 1961) and his Pasadena retrospective exhibition (October 8–November 3, 1963) are mentioned.*

The list does not match with either the readymades mentioned in his talk, nor with those shown in Pasadena. "In Advance of the broken arm" *and* "... Pliant ... de voyage" *were on display in Pasadena but are not part of this list.*

On the right "nouvelle unité de longeur / voir papiers Paul" refers to the "3 Stoppages Étalon"–*which seem to have been added to the list in a second step.*

The dates given for "Fresh Widow," *for* "Why Not Sneeze, Rose Sélavy?," *for* "La Bagarre d'Austerlitz" *and* "L.H.O.O.Q." *are not correct.*

Pour la boîte 1914, vous trouverez je crois les textes exacts dans le livre de Sanouillet : MARCHAND DU SEL — Terrain Vague Paris

Pour les autres textes de la "Boîte de 1914", je ne suis pas sûr:

a) L'idéex de la Fabrication (déjà dans la "Boîte Verte").
b) - 3 exemplaires obtenus dans des conditions à peu près sembl....
c) Les 3 stoppages étalon sont le mètre diminué.
? d) Vive! les vêtements et le presse raquette.
e) Faire un tableau de hasard heureux ou malheureux...
? f) Eloignement. Contre le service militaire obligatoire...
? g) L'Electricité en large....
? h) Etant donné que...; si je suppose que je sois souffrant beaucoup.
i) On peut xxxx regarder voir...
? k) - On n'a que: pour femelle la pissotière et on en vit. -
l) Un Monde en Jaune. Le Pont des volumes....
m) Le jeu de tonneau est une très belle "sculpture" d'adresse...
? n) Arrhe est à art ce que merdre est à merde....
o) La perspective linéaire est un bon moyen pour représenter....
? p) Faire une armoire à glace (pour le tain)....
q) Faire un tableau de fréquence.

Pusiqu'il y a des textes sur les "Ready-mades", faudrait-il y inclure aussi quelques reproductions de "Ready-mades"? lesquelles?

a) Roue de vélo, 1913
b) Pharmacie, 1914
d) Porte-bouteilles, 1914
d) In advance of the broken arm, 1915
e) Peigne, 1916
f) A bruit secret, 1916
g) Porte-manteau, 1916
h) Trébuchet, 1916
i) Apolinère enameled, 1916-18
k) Fontaine, 1917

naturellement faire bien la distinction entre
- Boîte 34
- Boîte 14
- Paquet de ready-mades

Enclosure to a letter from Marcel Duchamp to Serge Stauffer, August 18, 1960, Serge Stauffer and Marcel Duchamp correspondence, addenda to the 100 questions Stauffer wrote to Duchamp in 1960; Staatsgalerie Stuttgart, Graphische Sammlung, Inv. Nr. D 1993/561, Brief 6,3

Stauffer asked Duchamp which of the 10 readymades listed should be reproduced in his projected book alongside Duchamp's notes and writings on the topic of the readymade. Duchamp does not respond to the list but emphasizes the difference between Stauffer's "Paquet de ready mades" and the texts from the "Green Box" *and the "Box of 1914" (mentioned in their correspondence before).*

READYMADE RECORD (I): WHERE DOES OUR INFORMATION ON THE READYMADES COME FROM?

All the information referred to above goes back to Marcel Duchamp in the end. So it appears advisable to look for answers to our unresolved questions from different sources—contemporary witnesses, books, and newspapers. Here we meet another dilemma: there are practically no reliable sources from the time of the first readymades. Only in the 1920s do we occasionally find descriptions of Duchamp's activities that still appear relevant, though these activities are never identified as artworks, and often the term readymade isn't even used.

Our earliest example is the passage from a literary text by the American writer William Carlos Williams, who intermittently visited the Arensbergs' salon: "One day Du Champs [sic] decided that his composition for that day would be the first thing that struck his eye in the first hardware store he should enter. It turned out to be a pickaxe which he bought and set up in his studio. This was his composition."[33] Some authors suspect that Williams confused the pickaxe with Duchamp's snow shovel.[34] In view of the liveliness of Williams' account, this

33 William Carlos Williams, "Dialogue: The Return of the Sun," in: *The Little Review*, vol. 5, № 11 [12], April 1919, p. 4.

34 Dickran Tashjian, *William Carlos Williams and the American Scene, 1920–1940*, New York 1978, p. 59.

appears rather doubtful. Maybe the piece remained a "composition for that day," which is why it's no longer known to us.

Similar to Williams, Charles Sheeler, who also belonged to the Arensberg circle, saw Duchamp's ready-mades as a kind of spontaneous gesture. In a book—admittedly published much later—he remembers long nights at the Arensbergs' salon: Surrounded by a group of interested onlookers, Duchamp would always think of small things to pass the time, which he called ready-mades: "a tin cup, a can opener, an egg-beater, a strainer, arranging these in irrelevant combinations to which he gave strange titles. His humor never took the form of jokes but twists of expression."[35] Sheeler's retrospection of readymades as arrangements is backed up by Duchamp's notes that were published posthumously and include the following note in the section "Projets": "Without glue— / Make an assembly of 'ready mades' balanced one on the top of the other and photograph them (Jackstraws so to speak)."[36]

35 Quoted in: Constance Rourke, *Charles Sheeler: Artist in the American Tradition*, New York 1938 (reprint 1969), p. 48. On further appearances of the term 'ready-made' in texts by Ettie Stettheimer (1922) and Katherine Sophie Dreier (1923) see: Daniels, *Duchamp und die anderen*, pp. 186–194.

36 "Sans colle – Faire une réunion de 'ready mades' mis les uns au-dessus des autres en équilibre et photographier (Jackstraws

Information on the readymades reached Europe only in the context of Surrealism. In a short, euphoric text from 1922 dedicated to Duchamp, André Breton wrote: "But it is not the personality of choice [*personalité du choix*], the independence of which Duchamp, for example, by signing a manufactured object was one of the first to proclaim, the most tyrannical of all, and is it not fitting to put this to the test, provided that it is not to substitute for it a mysticism of chance?"[37] This is the first account mentioning that Duchamp signed his objects, yet Breton uses the term readymade no more than Williams does. Also, unlike the American contemporary witnesses from the circle of the Arensbergs, none of the French Surrealists can be considered a primary source. Their information most likely goes back to Duchamp's own statements and is not based on experience.

The readymades were not met with a more thorough critical appreciation until in the mid 1930s from writers

comme qui dirait)." Marcel Duchamp, *Notes: Préface par Pontus Hultén*, présentation et traduction par Paul Matisse, Paris, Centre National d'Art et de Culture Centre Pompidou 1980, № 167 (Thanks to Stefan Banz for pointing out this note to me)

37 André Breton, "Marcel Duchamp," in: *Litterature*, n.s. № 5, 1922, p. 8. English translation quoted in: Robert Motherwell (ed.), *The Dada Painters and Poets*, New York 1951, p. 210.

connected to Surrealism, but then they are often interpreted as provocations in the manner of Dadaism. Georges Hugnet, for example, wrote in 1932: "The 'simple thing' is consecrated, it is put on the pedestal of old and modern masterpieces indiscriminately thrown into the same bag, and art has no chance but to accept everything, it is enchained, forced to remain impotent."[38] "Pedestal" stands for the presentation in an exhibition, and yet at that point in time practically none of the readymades had actually been put on that pedestal. The double misunderstanding of the readymade as a scandalous object and as an exhibit in an art exhibition, which partly still persists today, begins with this text.

38 Georges Hugnet, "L'Esprit Dada dans la peinture" (part 1), in: *Cahiers d'Art*, № 1, 1932, pp. 64–65. Hugnet mentions the following readymades and dates: *Bottle Dryer* (1912), *Bicycle Wheel* (1913), "Fountain" (1917), *Snow Shovel, ... Pliant ... de voyage*, wardrobe hook from lathed wood. Apart from "*Fountain*" he doesn't mention titles or inscriptions. Surprisingly he doesn't mention the Mona Lisa, "*L.H.O.O.Q.*," or "*Pharmacie*," although both of them were exhibited in Paris a short time before, in an exhibition of collages organized by Louis Aragon: *La Peinture au défi*, Galerie Goemans, 1930. This suggests that both pieces were not then seen as readymades, but as drawings or collages.

A more differentiated view of the readymades became accessible only when Duchamp decided to review his own artistic past and feed it to the public in small doses. He did so in a highly artistic fashion with the *Green Box*, published in 1934,[39] and *Boîte-en-valise*, created between 1936 and 1941. For these boxes, Duchamp was the artist, author, editor, curator, producer, publisher, and gallerist all in one. It is hardly necessary to point out the meticulousness of these editions. For the first time they documented the full variety of Duchamp's work, and with their help he took full control over its reception history.

Almost everything that we know about the readymades today, we know from Marcel Duchamp himself. Yet from whom else could we possibly learn anything additional? In a "personal experiment," the supervisor determines the test setup and evaluates the results. In a way we therefore must rely on Duchamp's sincerity.

Yet could there be reasons to doubt Duchamp's statements? As scarce as other accounts from contemporary witnesses are, they verify all the main issues beyond such doubt: the catalog published at Bourgeois Galleries in 1916 proves that Duchamp coined the term readymade

39 André Breton and especially Gabrièle Buffet-Picabia published the first adequate appreciations of the readymade in the 1930s, for which they drew on the artist's notes in the *Green Box* and other statements by Duchamp. Before *Boîte-en-valise*, they had no other sources, and they had not seen the works themselves.

for a category of his works soon after his arrival in New York. Documents that have turned up only posthumously, such as his correspondence on the *Bottle Dryer* with Suzanne Duchamp, exactly match the particulars as Duchamp has related them. Before this letter was known, the *Bottle Dryer* might still have been a fake, since there were no direct sources proving the existence of this object—only when the letter became accessible in 1982 did we receive conclusive evidence that the piece existed, plus the additional value of an attempt to create a readymade retroactively and at a distance.[40]

40 The letters were in the possession of Alice Buckles-Brown and bequeathed to the Archives of American Art, Smithsonian Institution, Washington, D.C., on initiative of Francis Naumann. First publication in: Francis M. Naumann, "Affectueusement, Marcel: Ten Letters from Marcel Duchamp to Suzanne Duchamp and Jean Crotti," *Archives of American Art Journal*, vol. 22, № 4, 1982, pp. 2–19.

READYMADE TYPOLOGY: WHAT DO THE READYMADES HAVE IN COMMON?

Admittedly Duchamp's works and words have not yet given us a conclusive answer to the simple questions posed at the beginning of this book. Neither the extent of the readymades, nor the exact beginnings of Duchamp's readymade activities, have been fully clarified.

So do we know any better now what we are talking about when we discuss "the readymades" in their plural form? The artist's own comments give us no hope for a simple solution. A look at the art-historical and theoretical literature can similarly leave us disheartened: despite a number of voluminous and meticulously edited publications, so far we see no prospective consensus on establishing an exact corpus or a precise, comprehensive definition of the readymade. Experts in the field, who have engaged with Duchamp's oeuvre for many years, still arrive at surprisingly different selections of readymades.[41]

41 See, among others, the very different compilations by: André Gervais, "Liste des Readymades de Marcel Duchamp," pp. 122–125. This list has 56 entries over a period of 54 years and can serve as a touchstone for all encyclopedic attempts at a catalogue raisonné. Cf. also: André Gervais, *La Raie alitée d'effets*, p. 83. Dominique Chateau and Michel Vanpeene, "Catalogue raisonné des readymades I,"

So, to find a way out of this confusion, let us try and develop an independent set of criteria from the information that Duchamp has offered us. The artist himself seems to warn us when he says: "The strange thing about readymades is that I've never been able to come up with a definition or an explanation that fully satisfies me."[42] Let us nevertheless try.

READYMADE CRITERIA:

READYMADES ARE SIGNED.

- *The Bicycle Wheel*, Paris 1913, was not signed, its replica from 1916 in New York probably wasn't either.
- *The Bottle Dryer*, Paris 1914, was not yet signed—only in 1916, by way of a letter to his sister Suzanne, did Duchamp attempt to make it a "readymade at a distance" (his instructions could not be carried out).
- The urinal "*Fountain*" in 1917 was not signed by Duchamp, or at least not with the artist's name (instead it was signed "R. Mutt").

in: *Étant donné Marcel Duchamp*, № 1, premier semestre, 1999 (discontinued in 2005). Hector Obalk, "The Unfindable Readymade," in: *tout-fait,* vol. 1, № 2, May 2000, http://toutfait.com/issues/issue_2/Articles/obalk.html.

42 Katharine Kuh, *The Artist's Voice: Talks with Seventeen Artists*, New York 1962, p. 91.

- We do not know if "*Trébuchet*," "*... Pliant... de voyage*," or the *Hat Rack* were signed in 1917.[43]

READYMADES ARE TITLED AND / OR HAVE AN INSCRIPTION.

Three objects have no title (and no inscription), but only a descriptive name:

- *Bicycle Wheel*, Paris 1913 (Duchamp first started inscribing the objects in New York in 1915)
- *Bottle Dryer*, Paris 1914 (it did not receive its intended inscription in 1916)
- *Hat Rack*, New York 1917 (despite its creation in New York, there is no recorded inscription for this readymade)

On the other hand, there are titles and inscriptions recorded for objects that no longer exist or that remain unknown, for example "*Emergency in favor of twice*," which Duchamp mentions in the letter to his sister from January 1916.[44]

43 Schwarz in his *Complete Works* notes that all three readymades are "probably neither signed nor dated."

44 In Duchamp's own words (with underlined formatting by the artist): "Un autre 'readymade' s'appelle: Emergency in favor of twice, traduction française possible: Danger (Crise) en faveur de 2 fois." ("Another 'readymade' is called: Emergency in favor of twice, possible French translation: Danger (Crise) en faveur de 2 fois." Naumann and Obalk, *Affect[t] Marcel*, p. 43f.)

(EXCURSUS)

The way that an object is combined with language in the readymades would be worth a much longer study—especially in view of our difficult search for criteria. Let us here point to Duchamp's adoption of the English language for his titles, and the wordplay in some of them. In the letter to Suzanne Duchamp from January 1916 he writes: "I sign them and I think of an inscription for them in English."[45]

Again, we will find exceptions from the rule: *Comb* (from 1915) carries an inscription in French; the title of the lost object "*Pulled at Four Pins*" from 1915 is based on a senseless translation of a French figure of speech, and later an etching of the object from 1964 accordingly carries both an English and a French title; the work "*À Bruit secret*" / "*With Hidden Noise*" from 1916—labeled as a *readymade aidé* by Duchamp in *Boîte-en-valise*—uses complicated processes of translation between English and French; the two windows, "*Fresh Widow*" (1920) and "*La Bagarre d'Austerlitz*" (1921), play on English, or French, double meanings, which after 1920 become mostly the responsibility of Duchamp's female alter ego, Rrose Sélavy. Combining objects with titles and texts in two different languages, Duchamp established an interlingual culture of translation and transformation. The "verbal color" shines in many different hues.[46]

45 Ibid.

46 Interview Collin 1967, p. 38. Cf. also John C. Welchman, *Invisible Colors: A Visual History of Titles*, New Haven et al. 1997, pp. 219–231, for a general discussion of Duchamp's work titles.

READYMADES ARE SERIALLY MANUFACTURED UTILITY OBJECTS.

Of the eight objects described by Duchamp as pure readymades in Boîte-en-valise, two do not match this criterion:

- "*Pharmacie*," 1914, is an art print and not a utility object.
- "*Air de Paris*," 1919, was hand-sealed by a pharmacist on behalf of Duchamp, so it was not manufactured serially, it was made "on-demand" instead of waiting to be purchased "ready-made."

Duchamp explained the difference between the readymade and the surrealist *objet trouvé*: "Most of my readymades were mass produced and could be duplicated."[47] Conversely, this means that not all of them were mass produced products, as Duchamp was ready to admit: "'*Pharmacie*' was manufactured only to a certain degree."[48]

The objects that Duchamp described as a *readymade aidé* or *readymade rectifié* do not match the criterion any better than the objects and assemblages

47 Interview Kuh, 1961, p. 91f.

48 Schwarz, *Collected Works*, p. 597. On the differentiation between artistic craftsmanship, serially manufactured goods (such as the bottle dryers and snow shovels in Duchamp's time), and industrial machine production, see: Lars Blunck, *Duchamps Readymade*, Munich 2017, especially chapter 2, "Werke nach dem Handwerk."

made after 1920 under the name of Rrose Sélavy. André Breton was already conscious of this problem, as we can gather from a quick revision of his attempt at defining the readymades. In 1934 he speaks of "manufactured objects" that could be "promoted to the dignity of objects of art through the choice of the artist."[49] Four years later, in the *Dictionnaire abrégé du Surréalisme* by Breton and Paul Éluard, the objet *manufacture* is replaced by objet *usuel*, or "utility object."[50] This shift, from the production to the application of the object, fundamentally changes the meaning of Breton's often quoted definition.

Some of Duchamp's recorded ideas and activities have the characteristics of a gesture. A note from 1916 reads: "Find inscription for Woolworth Bldg. as readymade."[51] So is the Woolworth building—which at the time was the tallest building in the world—now part of

49 André Breton, "Phare de la mariée," in: *Minotaure*, № 6, winter 1934 / 35, p. 46: "Objets manufacturés promus à la dignité d'objets d'art par le choix de l'artiste." English translation: André Breton, "Lighthouse of the Bride," in: *View. The Modern Magazine*, Marcel Duchamp Number, series V, № 1, 1945, p. 7.

50 André Breton and Paul Éluard (eds.), *Dictionnaire abrégé du Surréalisme*, Paris 1938, p. 23: "Objet usuel promu à la dignité..."

51 Sanouillet and Peterson, *The Essential Writings of Marcel Duchamp*, p. 75.

Duchamp's oeuvre? A wall painting of a battle scene in the New York Café des Artistes, spontaneously signed by Duchamp during a dinner party, has indeed found its way into his catalog of works.[52] And regarding some of the notes Duchamp included in his *Green Box* from 1934, we do not know if they ever were realized, e.g.: "Buy a pair of Ice-tongs as Rdymde."[53] One famous example that was certainly never realized is: "Reciprocal Readymade = Use a Rembrandt as an ironing board."[54]

(EXCURSUS)

Like his combinations of objects and language, Duchamp's purely verbal or literary readymades would also merit a more thorough digression. In 1918 Duchamp mentions: "A very funny article in the Tribune is a 'Readymade.' I signed it, but didn't write it."[55] Later, in the 1920s, there are "*Ventilation*" (a text taken from an information

52 Schwarz, Collected Works, № 341.
53 Sanouillet and Peterson, *The Essential Writings of Marcel Duchamp*, p. 33.
54 Ibid., p. 32.
55 Duchamp in a letter to the Stettheim sisters (Thomas Girst, *The Duchamp Dictionary*, London 2014, p. 155). Duchamp comments on an article in The New York Tribune, September 12, 1915 written by Henry McBride but, "Marcel Duchamp" is credited as the author. (see facsimile and comment by Francis Naumann in: Philapdelphia Museum of Art Bulletin, No. 328, 1980, p. 13).

sign in New York taxis, published under Duchamp's name in the magazine *New York Dada* in 1921),[56] "*The Non-Dada*" (a booklet containing a religious pamphlet, titled and signed by Duchamp in 1922),[57] and finally the apocryphal text "Man Before the Mirror" (published under Duchamp's name in a Man Ray catalog from 1934).[58]

These texts appropriated by Duchamp have rarely been examined; they are not even mentioned in most literature on the readymade. Only "*The Non-Dada*" has found entry into Arturo Schwarz's exhaustive work catalog, despite Schwarz's lengthy discursion on the prehistory of the "printed Readymade" starting with Lautréamont and Baudelaire.[59]

Largely unknown, the poet Blaise Cendrars also chose a "ready-made" artwork in 1914, the year of Duchamp's *Bottle Dryer*, when he copied his poem *Dernière Heure* from the eponymous newspaper column in *Paris Midi* nearly word for word.[60]

56 Sanouillet and Peterson, *The Essential Writings of Marcel Duchamp*, p. 179; not in Schwarz's Complete Works.

57 Schwarz, *Complete Works*, № 402.

58 Sanouillet and Peterson, *The Essential Writings of Marcel Duchamp*, p. 188f.

59 Schwarz, *Complete Works*, p. 50f.

60 On the small changes that Cendrars made to the original report, see Jean-Pierre Goldenstein, *Dix-neuf poèmes élastiques de Blaise Cendrars*, Paris 1986, p. 74.

READYMADES WERE CHOSEN BY MARCEL DUCHAMP.

This criterion is at the heart of André Breton's initial attempt at defining the readymade and it has remained a standard until today. And yet even this very obvious fact can be questioned. In the early period of the readymades, Duchamp delegates central tasks to others:

- In 1916 the signing of the *Bottle Dryer* to his sister Suzanne (without success).
- Also in 1916, the choice of whatever is hidden inside "*À Bruit secret*," thus eliciting the "secret noise" of the title, to Walter Arensberg.
- In 1919 the realization of the "*Readymade malheureux*" to his sister Suzanne, whom he sends instructions from Buenos Aires.

This practice of delegating continues in the 1950s. Several objects, authorized and exhibited by Duchamp, were chosen by others: the urinal for the first exhibition of "*Fountain*" in New York in 1950 was selected by the gallerist Sidney Janis. Further versions of the urinal were selected by others in 1953 and 1963, as were some of the *Bottle Dryers* signed by Duchamp after 1960. In an especially amusing letter from 1962, Duchamp advises Werner Hofmann to buy from the *Bazar de l'Hôtel de Ville* department store an appropriate bottle dryer for the permanent exhibition at the Museum Moderne Kunst in Vienna.[61] This bottle dryer bears no sig-

61 Earlier, Werner Hofmann had loaned a signed version from Duchamp for the exhibition *Kunst von 1900 bis heute*, which was afterward returned to

nature or inscription and today is in the collection of the Hamburger Kunsthalle, where Hofmann became the director in 1969.[62] In this way, after the failed attempt of 1916, Duchamp's project of a "readymade at a distance," authorized by letter, finally came into existence.

The debate on the authorship of "*Fountain*," which has flamed up again and again since the 1980s, also traces back to a letter from Marcel to Suzanne Duchamp. It is dated April 11, 1917, two days after the opening of the "Independents." Duchamp writes: "A female friend of mine, using a male pseudonym, Richard Mutt, submitted a porcelain urinal as a sculpture."[63] In the secondary literature, a couple of illustrious candidates are brought up for whom that woman may have been: Louise Norton (translator of French poetry, later the wife and biographer of composer Edgar Varèse) and Elsa von Freytag-Loringhoven (an eccentric, precarious total artist, long

Duchamp. The artist's letter from Christmas Day 1962 is an answer to Hofmann's request for another replica of the *Bottle Dryer* as a permanent exhibit. See the facsimile of the letter in: Dieter Daniels and Alfred M. Fischer, *Übrigens sterben immer die anderen: Marcel Duchamp und die Avantgarde seit 1950*, Cologne 1988, p. 76.

62 Hamburger Kunsthalle, inv. № 1987 / 2. Interestingly, this replica has been left out of Schwarz's work catalog.

63 Naumann and Obalk, *Affect^t Marcel*, p. 47.

unrecognized author of the assemblage "*God*").[64] Even if a conspiracy theory had gone viral in roughly 2012, saying that Duchamp—covered by the art establishment—had later taken possession of what was originally Elsa von Freytag-Loringhoven's urinal: art is not a whodunit, and the readymade is not a murder but, following Duchamp, a rendezvous.[65]

64 Cf. the detailed studies on "*Fountain*" by William A. Camfield, *Marcel Duchamp: Fountain*, Houston 1989; Heinz Herbert Mann, *Marcel Duchamp: 1917*, Munich 1999; Irene Gammel, *Baroness Elsa: Gender, Dada, and Everyday Modernity—A Cultural Biography*, Cambridge 2002; Michael R. Taylor, *Marcel Duchamp. The Great Hidden Inspirer*, Berlin 2017 (chapter: "Blind Man's Bluff")

65 The mastermind behind these conspiracy theories is Glyn Thompson; see the announcement for his recent publication: "The de-attribution of the urinal from Duchamp's oeuvre, and its consequent attribution to that of Elsa von Freytag-Loringhoven, completely overturns establishment orthodoxy by reconfiguring the disposition of evidence hitherto marginalized and suppressed in the sustaining of the dominant myths of the Duchamp master narrative." Advertisement for Glyn Thompson, *Duchamp's*

What mode of authorship could be deemed legitimate in a situation as unclear as our search for criteria has demonstrated? What departure from such a mode could be denounced as an illegitimate appropriation? It seems futile to make a decision here, on the one hand because of the unclear criteria for the authorship of a readymade, on the other hand due to the scarcity of sources.

Urinal? The Facts behind the Façade,
Leeds 2015, http://wildpansypress.com.

READYMADE RECORD (II): ARE THERE ANY UNKNOWN READYMADES?

Since our information on the readymades comes almost exclusively from Marcel Duchamp, it appears dubious to ask for any "unknown readymades." Instead we might ask: Is it maybe possible that—quite apart from the sincerity of Duchamp's statements we have to rely on—he selected more readymades than are known to us today (mostly through Duchamp's own testimony)?

We have already found clear evidence of that. A readymade unknown today, titled "*Emergency in favor of twice*," is mentioned in the letter to Suzanne Duchamp from January 1916—proof that an object must have disappeared. A reference to a ready-made newspaper article signed by Duchamp can be found in a letter to the Stettheim sisters. Then there are written documents by others: We do not know the pickaxe whose selection was described by William Carlos Williams, nor the little arrangements described by Charles Sheeler.

Besides this evidence in writing, there are also visual traces of objects, and we can easily speculate if these should be counted among the core group of readymades. On the upper right side of Duchamp's 1918 photograph of shadows thrown by readymades titled "*Ombres Portées*" we see, overlapping with "*À Bruit secret*," another object that has not yet been identified. There are more traces, e.g. the shadow of a corkscrew appearing in Duchamp's last painting on canvas "*Tu 'm*" from 1918 next to the shadow of a bicycle wheel and a hat rack. Together these titles without surviving objects and these shadows of objects without recorded titles have a mysterious charm, adding an aura of vagueness and inconceivability to the core group of readymades.

Presumably the artist applied his directive from the *Green Box*, noted down during the time when he created the readymades, even more rigidly in retrospect: "Limit the no. of rdymades yearly..."[66] Duchamp deliberately kept the extent of his readymade project open, as proven by the fact that e.g. another note in the *Green Box* of 1934, "Buy a pair of Ice-tongs as Rdymde," has left no trace in the *Boîte-en-valise*, which was compiled a short time later.[67] The belated addition of an etching showing a chimney ventilator, titled "*Pulled at Four Pins*," to the edition of "14 Readymades" likewise calls the finality of their selection into question.

In this overview of the readymades that no longer exists as objects, we find a very idiosyncratic variety of records: a title accidentally found in a letter, a work note later published in the *Green Box*, a painted shadow, and finally a graphic that remembers a titled object. These very diverse references appear just as carefully measured, even orchestrated, as the multifarious objects known as readymades that we have encountered above.

Which leads us to a tentative summary: There is no standard mode for the readymade record, just as there is none for their inventory or their chronology. The readymades are not a closed, clearly defined group of works, but a historical activity whose modes of articu-

66 Sanouillet and Peterson, *The Essential Writings of Marcel Duchamp*, p. 33.
67 Ibid.

lation are just as various as their historical record. This record involves anything from surviving originals (*Comb*), through texts (*Green Box*), or documentations (*Boîte-en-valise*) offered to us by the artist, up to letters and other contemporary sources as hidden evidence.

Some of this evidence seems to suggest that Duchamp filtered the record, highlighting certain examples, mentioning others only casually or not at all. And yet it would be wrong to see this as an act of concealment. Duchamp never pretended to deliver a comprehensive historical documentation with *Boîte-en-valise* or the edition of "14 Readymades"—and no one ever asked him if he intended to.

Instead of a filtering of the object record, we can speak of an experimental try-out of different modes of making. Some ideas remain in a purely conceptual state—such as the notes on the "reciprocal readymade" or on finding a title (probably never implemented) for the Woolworth Building. On the other hand, Duchamp repeatedly mentioned his spontaneous signing of the wall painting depicting a battle scene at a café in New York.[68] Lars Blunck has accordingly suggested that we might understand the readymade as an expansion of artistic methods that has more of the characteristics of a "practice" or a "gesture" than of an "object."[69]

68 Schwarz, *Complete Works*, № 341. André Breton speaks of the "gesture of signing some big, decorative painting in a restaurant." (Breton, "Phare de la mariée," p. 46.)

69 See for more detail: Lars Blunck,

If we compare the gestures of Duchamp to the art of the 1960s (that in many ways referred to him), we can speak of an artistic approach that sometimes materializes in an object, but generally can take different forms. The canonical exhibition title *When Attitudes Become Form* applies here quite literally.

(EXCURSUS) DUCHAMP AS CURATOR (OF THE READYMADES)?

Recently Duchamp is being discovered as a curator.[70]

Duchamps Readymade, Munich 2017. Blunck's important study argues against the "objectivist" misunderstanding of the readymade as "a utility object consecrated as a work of art, and thus an object-like exhibit." He develops the idea of the readymade as an "artistic practice," which is not bound to objects, but just as well contains gestures, concepts, processes, and linguistic elements.

70 Cf. *Duchamp as Curator. Marcel Duchamp's Curatorial Practice: His Work, Contemporary Exhibitions, Museums, Private Collections and Publications*, ed. by Renate Wiehager and Katharina Neuburger, Cologne 2017. We have to distinguish between a curatorial practice in relation to Duchamp's own work or that of others, since he organized exhibitions by Brancusi, Picabia, and others to settle his livelihood. To the latter category also

Especially so are the readymades that are understood as "curatorial gestures."[71] Elena Filipovic writes: "Duchamp's so-called invention of the readymade must itself be qualified, and the little-discussed, but more labored and layered, set of activities that were crucial in historically positioning the readymade must be highlighted. In this telling, the readymade is not only an object selected and nominated but, perhaps even more importantly, one that is curated."[72]

The performative aspect of the readymade—also examined by Lars Blunck—complements the history of objects that has been our focus so far. Nevertheless, such concepts of the readymade as a "curatorial construction,"[73] undertaken by the artist himself, presuppose a publicity that was simply not extant during the

belongs his engagement for the *Société Anonyme, Inc.*—later receiving the explanatory addendum *Museum of Modern Art: 1920*—founded by Duchamp with Katherine Dreier and Man Ray (cf. Katharina Neuburger, *Die amerikanische Erfahrung, oder: Weshalb Marcel Duchamp in New York Werke ausstellen konnte, die keine Kunst sind*, Cologne 2017).

71 Elena Filipovic, *The Apparently Marginal Activities of Marcel Duchamp*, Cambridge, MA, and London 2016, p. 76. On Duchamp's understanding of exhibiting the readymades as "tests," see ibid.,. p. 77.

72 Ibid., p. 6.

73 Ibid., p. 76.

decisive years between 1914 and 1917. When Duchamp tested possible forms of presentation for his readymades between 1916 and 1917, these tests were failures in the sense that the public either did not notice or that they outright misunderstood them. Conversely, the tests were successful within the parameters of Duchamp's experiment, whose objective the artist formulated in a note from 1913 when he asked: "Can one make works which are not works of 'art'?"[74]

On the other hand, the role of the curator could be described as another form of "making with the readymade" (Blunck on the readymade). The curator "makes" an exhibition out of artworks that others (the artists) have already made, or will make for the occasion. Curators work with things that are unambiguously coded as art. If they sometimes integrate utility objects into an art exhibition as a commentary or reference, they do it to emphasize their difference from art—strengthening the distinction between art and non-art that Marcel Duchamp with his readymades had wanted to revoke.

Duchamp once called the art collector an "artist squared."[75] In similar fashion, the curator is an author

74 Sanouillet and Peterson, *The Essential Writings of Marcel Duchamp*, p. 74.

75 "There are all sorts of collectors: the real collector—the one I oppose to the commercial collectors who have made modern art a field comparable to a Wall Street affair—the real collector, in my opinion, is an artist *au carré*; he selects paintings and puts them on his wall, in other words, 'he

figure on the meta level of art and—like the collector—has become much more of a celebrity over the last decades. In contrast, during the years of 1914 to 1917, Duchamp's readymades operated below the perception threshold of the art world. Duchamp did not appear as an author figure, instead he tried to shift authorship from the production side to that of the reception of the objects. His experiment started out as a personal affair, before it was published in homeopathic doses over the next 50 years, to set a process in motion at the end of which, according to Duchamp, the spectators make the art. The current popularity of the readymade can be seen as proof of his conviction, formulated in 1956, that "a work is made entirely by those who look at it or read it and who make it survive by their accolades or even their condemnation."[76] Of course, among that audience we also find curators, collectors, conservators, art historians, and especially a host of other artists, who since the second half of the 20th century have advanced the canonization of the readymade. In a readymade context, Duchamp would be less a curator of his own work, but

paints a collection.'" (Marcel Duchamp at the Western Round Table of Modern Art, San Francisco 1949, transcript ed. by Douglas MacAgy, section D, p. 38, online at http://ubu.com/historical/wrtma/transcript_d/pages/38.htm.)

76 Marcel Duchamp in a letter dated 1956 to Jean Mayoux, published in: Jean Mayoux *La Liberté une et divisible: Textes critiques et politiques*, Ussel 1979.

rather a curator squared, an artist who, as it were, curates the reception history of his oeuvre. More simply, we might say he is "nothing else but an artist"—though surely an artist who coordinated and controlled the historical impact of his work.[77]

SUMMARY READYMADE TYPOLOGY: There Is No Precise, Comprehensive Definition of "the Readymades" by Marcel Duchamp

Just as we have expected, our attempt at finding a set of our own criteria for a typology of "the readymades" by Marcel Duchamp has been as unsuccessful as our earlier attempts at establishing a chronology or nomenclature. We have expected this outcome not just because of the artist's own warning that he had never been able to find a satisfactory definition for the readymades, but also since comparable attempts in the scholarly literature have brought no result. The various definitions and criteria usually arrived at are incompatible with each other and only tend to make things more confusing.

Behind our failure, though, lurks a question of method, or maybe we should say: a methodical trap. All

77 Unpublished interview with Richard Hamilton and Katharine Kuh, 1961, quoted in: Calvin Tomkins, *Duchamp. A Biography*, New York 1966, p. 416.

attempts at a definition are refuted by certain exceptions to the rule, exceptions that have been legitimized as readymades by Duchamp himself. This is why an inventory of the readymades cannot succeed—it would first require a set of criteria. In other words: no inventory without a definition... and no definition without an inventory, a perfect aporia.

POSTSCRIPT: READYMADE DERIVATES

While searching for criteria that may get us closer to a definition of "the readymades" by Marcel Duchamp, we have confined ourselves to the pure readymades from the period between 1914 and 1917. If we wanted to take into account all derivates of the readymade from after 1919, then the situation would still be more confusing. Some of these were introduced by Duchamp himself: *readymade rectifié*, *readymade aidé*, and *semi-readymade*. Additional categories have been offered in the secondary literature (*readymade latent* and *readymade provoqué* by Arturo Schwarz; *printed readymade* and *imitated rectified readymade* by Francis Naumann; or the more elaborate terminology of a *readymade imité aidé corrigeé* by André Gervais).[78]

Also, we have not taken the renewal of Duchamp's readymade activities at the end of the 1950s into con-

78 See the selections in: Schwarz, *Complete Works*, p. 44f.; Naumann, *The Art of Making Art in the Age of Mechanical Reproduction*, p. 298f; Gervais, "Liste des Readymades de Marcel Duchamp."

sideration, since it would need a separate analysis. Autonomous readymade works by Duchamp (for example a series of men's waistcoats with names on their buttons from 1957 and 1958,[79] or a Spanish greeting card titled "*Pollyperruque*" from 1967[80]) would have to be differentiated from casual signings of objects offered to him by friends and acquaintances, to which he sometimes added puns as titles (e.g. "*Signed Sign*," 1963,[81] or "*Faux Vagin*," 1962–63[82])—and of course these distinctions again could not be made with absolute certainty. The casual signings are a play on the value of Duchamp's signature, which accumulated over the history of the readymade, they are a postscript under the conditions of canonization and commercialization.

From this context, we also expressly exclude all attempts at a posthumous valorization of objects before 1913 that Duchamp signed with a dedication.[83] This

79 Schwarz, *Complete Works*, № 554.
80 Ibid., № 644.
81 Ibid., № 587.
82 Ibid., № 663.
83 The wooden toy, which in French is called a *Bilboquet* belongs here. It carries the dedication "Bilboquet / Souvenir de Paris / A mon ami M. Bergmann / Duchamp printemps 1910" and was shown in the exhibition *The Bilboquet Room, Marcel Duchamp*, Moeller Fine Art Ltd. Berlin, December 12, 2011, to January 26, 2012, as Duchamp's first readymade.

inflation of the artist's consistently limited number of readymades is motivated by mercantile interests and dilutes a central core of the original idea: Duchamp's refusal to succumb to the pressure for repetitions desired especially by the art market.

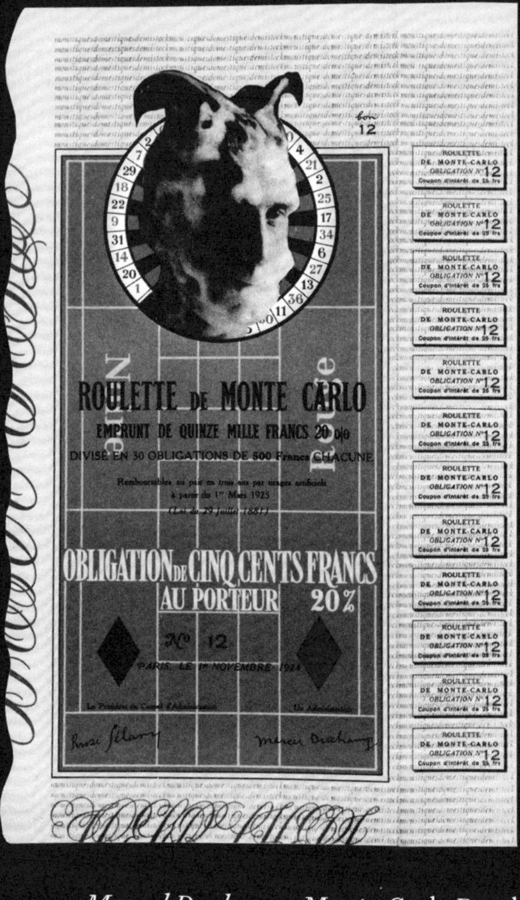

Marcel Duchamp, Monte Carlo Bonds, *1924, (as reproduced in the* Boîte-en-valise*). Labeled as "imitated rectified Readymade" (Arturo Schwarz) or as "readymade imité aidé corrigeé" (André Gervais).*

SUMMARY READYMADE INDEX:

The Aporia of the Readymade

What follows from the aporia of the readymade? Does it mean that after a hundred years we stand empty-handed at the centennial of the readymade? Can we continue speaking of "the readymades" of Duchamp in the plural seemingly as a matter of fact, without knowing what exactly we mean?

Maybe we just have to change perspectives. Maybe the failure of our attempt to find a definition or constant criteria for readymades must be seen as Duchamp's biggest achievement.

So let us put Duchamp's comments to another close reading. This time we take the liberty of condensing his statements which he varies from one interview to the next. We can take him at his word when he summarizes the internal logic of his work: "I have forced myself to contradict myself in order to avoid conforming to my own taste."[84] And on the selection of the readymades: "If you're looking for a central idea, then no... I could have chosen 20 things per hour, and in the end they would have all looked the same. That's absolutely not what I wanted."[85]

84 Harriet and Sidney Janis, "Marcel Duchamp Anti-Artist," in *View*, vol. 5, № 1, March 1945, p. 258.

85 Interview, Hahn, 1966b, p. 61. Cf. also his remark: "Slowly! A readymade now and then, but not ten per day." Interview

The limited number of the readymades is also a precondition for their diversity. This is not an automatic result of the artist's selection, instead, it proved "a difficult task" not to follow his own personal taste, as Duchamp confided.[86] And in a double questioning of himself he added: "I'm not at all sure that the concept of the readymade isn't the most important single idea to come out of my work."[87]

Duchamp casually stated the principle of a purposeful difference, a non-consistency, a disparity, as we have by now gathered in our somewhat laborious way. In the BBC television interview mentioned above, he said a few months before his death: "So the choice came only for a few objects quite disparate, disparate and different from one another, enough so that today, looking at the thirteen readymades I made in the course of thirty years, maybe, I'm satisfied by the fact that this is... they don't look like one another. You see what I mean? In other words, there is a different, completely [sic] strangeness from one to the other, which shows there is no style there."[88]

Charbonnier, 1960–1961.

86 Interview Kuh 1961, p. 92.

87 Ibid.

88 Interview Bakewell, 1968, p.304. Cf. the similar statement in an interview with Werner Spies, 1967: "The fact that even today, after 50 years, there is no unity, no similarity between the different readymades, proves that I have not been attracted by formal charms." (Stauffer,

Is that all there is? What remains as the result of our efforts? Is it revealed that in the end, in the words of Duchamp, "there is no solution because there is no problem?"[89]

If the strategic aim in choosing the readymades was that of a difference, an inconsistency, that already would explain the need to limit their number. In all probability, Duchamp continued to reduce the number of chosen objects, of related gestures and ideas, before he made the readymades and his accompanying notes available to the public. In the final analysis, the "art" is probably less in the choice of a single object and more in the arrangement of a complete ensemble. So if we talk about "the readymades" of Duchamp, there is an additional meaning that is given: it is not just a generic term, but designates a thoroughly composed group, in which every object takes on a specific role. So, in allusion to Latour's idea of a "parliament of things,"[90] we could almost speak of an orchestra of things.

It is in this sense that Duchamp compares choosing the readymades to the making of the *Large Glass*: "Yes, I introduced again very elaborate decisions about details, even in the readymades. The fact that it was not made with my hands didn't stop me from finding other ways of applying my meticulous technique to

Interviews und Statements, p. 232.)

89 Janis and Janis, "Marcel Duchamp Anti-Artist," p. 265.

90 Introduced in Bruno Latour, *We Have Never Been Modern*, Cambridge, MA, 1993.

them, you see? In spite of myself, I'm a meticulous man..."[91]

The problem of talking about "the readymades" in the plural is mainly one of constructing an academic theory, as far as the theses of such a theory depend on generalizations. Any attempt at making statements about "the readymades" fails if we don't limit ourselves to a clearly defined group of them, because each of the objects displays a very specific combination of features (selection, inscription, fabrication, alteration, etc.). Which is why some of the more interesting and elegant theories on "the readymades" are often refuted, or at least questioned, by pointing to a counterexample from the same (often implicitly understood) group.[92]

91 Interview Hamilton / Hamilton 1959

92 Sebastian Egenhofer, for instance, has developed an interesting theory on the temporality of the readymade when he writes: "It has to be a serial product so that the beginning of its becoming does not blend with the time of its material production." As we have seen, in "*Air de Paris*," the object "becoming" a readymade definitely blends with its material production by the pharmacist who created it to Duchamp's instructions. See Sebastian Egenhofer, "The Becoming of the Readymade: The concept of the work of art after Duchamp," in: G. Ulrich Großmann and Petra Krutisch (eds.), *The*

To get out of this dilemma, there are two possibilities for speaking about readymades: we can talk specifics instead of generalizations, something which many monographic studies of single readymades have tried. The danger here is a discourse negotiated among specialists, so that the undeniable popular appeal of the readymade falls from view. The second possibility would be to speak in the plural, yet not about the readymades' lowest common denominator, but seeing them as the creation of an ensemble that cannot be homogenized by criteria or definitions. It means understanding Duchamp's readymades as a multiform, inherently complex, and heterogeneous practice, as a hybrid combination of diverse practices, which only all together unfold the enormous impact. This could be grasped only in the plural form and must always stay in the pluralistic—without a narrowed, simplified, canonized, and thus partly misconceived notion of the readymade.

If, like Duchamp himself, we cannot arrive at a definition, that does not mean the readymades have no common features. We talk about "the readymades" in the sense of a family resemblance, which connects them in a network, yet does not require common characteristics that would have to apply to all. According to Ludwig Wittgenstein, a family resemblance is what allows us to talk about an abstract term, even when we cannot define

Challenge of the Object, 33rd Congress of the International Committee of the History of Art, Congress Proceedings—Part 4, Nuremberg 2013, pp. 1228–1230.

equally valid criteria for all its aspects.[93] Within the readymade microcosm we meet the same problem as in the macrocosm of speaking about all art: we have no clear definition of "art," and yet we talk about it.

Instead of stabilizing the readymade by criteria or a definition, we have achieved something else entirely: we have maintained openness, interminability, non-con-

93 In the 1960s arose a theoretical debate on the definability of art which followed up on Wittgenstein's idea of the family resemblance. On the state of this debate, see: Francis Longworth and Andrea Scarantino, "The Disjunctive Theory of Art: The Cluster Account Reformulated," in: *British Journal of Aesthetics*, vol. 50, № 2, 2010, pp. 151–167. Apparently Wittgenstein's concept of a family resemblance is different from Duchamp's, since Duchamp explicitly rejected the idea of a family resemblance for the readymades if it was based on generalized characteristics that would be equally valid for all of them: "And it's because of this that all these readymades, in sum, are so different from one another... so different that there isn't, if you will... the air of a family about them... There isn't any air of family between *Pharmacy*, which we've spoken of, and the *Bottlerack* or the *Bicycle Wheel* that turns!" Interview Neyens, 1965.

ceivability. This is why the readymade is not an exception, it is a precedent: our futile attempts at a definition of the seemingly trivial object offers the best example for the general indefinability of art. In art, every rule has its exception, and at least since the advent of modernism this exception is often more important for further developments than the rule.

According to Duchamp, there is a second sense in which the readymade defies the definition of a work of art, as he explains in a relatively early interview from 1959, before the more widespread readymade reception by Pop art and Nouveau Réalisme set in: "Can we try to define art? We have tried, everybody has tried and in every century there is a new definition of art, meaning that there is no essential one... that is good for all centuries... So if we accept the idea of trying not to define art, which is a very legitimate conception, then the readymade can be seen as a sort of irony, because it says: here it is, a thing that I call art, I didn't even make it myself. And as is commonly known, art etymologically speaking means to 'make,' 'hand-make,' and there, instead of making it, I take it ready-made. So it was a form of denying the possibility of defining art... Because you don't define electricity, you just see the results of electricity, but you don't define it."[94]

In this multifaceted statement, Duchamp claims that readymades subvert the established definition of art as something that was made, because as works of

94 Interview Hamilton / Hamilton 1959.

art they are the exception from this definition.[95] Today of course we would need to update the artist's 1959 statement: After Duchamp, artistic practices that include the use of something "ready-made" have become part of a new definition of art in the 20th and 21st centuries. This is why we can no longer see the readymade as "denying the possibility of defining art" per se, in the way that Duchamp hopes it will. With the readymade begins a new form of artistic authorship, a form of making beyond manual creation, which has become part of the canon today.

Despite or maybe because of the fact that it proves impossible to find stable criteria for Duchamp's readymades, they have become an engine for changing the criteria of art. Which means that its conceptual openness and its many possible interpretations have become a central factor of the readymade's immense impact on the history of art (and its theory as well).

Accordingly, we can reformulate Duchamp's statement in view of art since the 1960s: One just sees the results of the readymade, but is unable to define it.[96]

95 Duchamp does not say that a definition for the readymades would be impossible, as is sometimes claimed for shorter versions of this quote.

96 Sebastian Egenhofer in this context speaks of a "work process" that is "never ready and finished, but open towards the future." He argues: "One could write a history of modernity by taking sections

Only because of this openness, a hundred years later it is still fascinating to engage with the readymades of Marcel Duchamp. It's why this book has been written and why you hold it in your hand.

through this line of projection of the readymade in which every fifteen years another meaning, another image seems to gain contours." (Sebastian Egenhofer, "Passages of the Object in the Art of Modernity," in: *Re-Object*, exh. cat. Kunsthaus Bregenz, ed. by Eckhard Schneider, Cologne 2007, p. 163f.)

II. READYMADE EXPOSITION[1]

1 Referring to a note by Duchamp, Sebastian Egenhofer sees the term exposition as "the decisive link between the terminology of the *Large Glass* and the readymades. I don't interpret 'exposition' as the measure of time in a photographic exposure (which is what Rosalind Krauss or Jean Clair do), but only as a point in time, more precisely the beginning of the infinite exposure of the readymade: its original date can be understood as the start of its exposition (dangling, collecting dust, being happenstanced by its reception)." Sebastian Egenhofer in an email to the author, November 22, 2016; cf. Sebastian Egenhofer, *Abstraktion—Kapitalismus—Subjektivität: Die Wahrheitsfunktion des Werks in der Moderne*, Munich 2008, p. 163f, and idem, *Produktionsaesthetik*, Zürich 2010, p. 84, note 11.

In the second half of the "Readymade Century," the readymades of Marcel Duchamp have found company: many other artists use strategies of "already made" objects in their exhibitions. From this change of context, the question of visibility in regards to Duchamp's lost objects must be asked anew.

DO READYMADES HAVE TO BE EXHIBITED?

Let us again start from seemingly simple questions—such as the viewer's personal experience with a work of art, a basic premise in the visual arts: Have you ever seen a readymade? Try to remember where and when you first encountered a readymade—what was the museum, the exhibition, the exact object(s) in question? We will return to this later.

If you have seen a readymade, it obviously must have been exhibited, that much appears self-evident. For a long time, its presentation in an exhibition was thus considered not merely a possibility, but a precondition for a readymade. Its "exposition" can therefore be seen as part of its "production" within an art context. In fact, some readers might have missed this criterion—that the readymades are exhibited—in the first part of this text.

For a long time, presentation within an exhibition appeared as part of the basic criteria for readymades in art theory. Up until now, many authors naturally

As early as 1915, in New York, Marcel Duchamp had given a foretaste of the principles of Dada by exhibiting the most ordinary and most preposterous objects, the so-called ready-mades, as works of art.

Phaidon Encyclopedia of Art and Artists, *London 1978, p. 148, entry: "Dada"*

BBC NEWS

Watch **One-Minute World News**

News Front Page

Africa
Americas
Asia-Pacific
Europe
Middle East
South Asia
UK
Business
Health
Science & Environment
Technology
Entertainment
Arts & Culture
Also in the news

Last Updated: Wednesday, 1 December, 2004, 17:56 GMT

E-mail this to a friend   Printable version

Duchamp's urinal tops art survey

A white gentlemen's urinal has been named the most influential modern art work of all time.

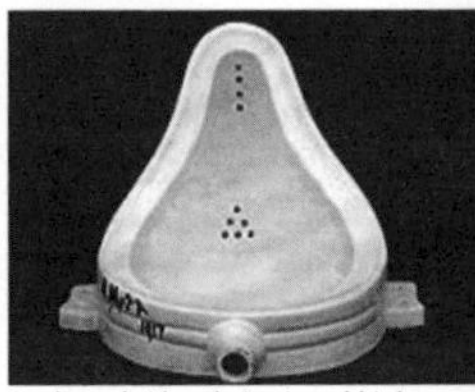

Duchamp's idea that art could take any form shocked the art world

Marcel Duchamp's Fountain came top of a poll of 500 art experts in the run-up to this year's Turner Prize which takes place on Monday.

Picasso's Les Demoiselles d'Avignon (1907) was second, with Andy Warhol's Marilyn Diptych from 1962 coming third.

Duchamp shocked the art establishment when he took the urinal, signed it and put it on display in 1917.

BBC One Minute World News, 1. December 2004

assumed that readymades had actually been exhibited at the time of their creation.[2] In the 1970s they served as a prime example of institutional art theory, which argued that their transfer into the institutional framework of an art context constituted a decisive difference between readymades and everyday objects.[3]

Duchamp, however, repeatedly pointed to the fact that for a long time he did not exhibit the readymades. He said to Calvin Tomkins in 1964: "Never did I show them. Nobody saw them until twenty years ago."[4] Furthermore, in the interview from 1965, already quoted above, Duchamp unambiguously assured us that the readymades were a "very personal experiment" that he "never expected to show to the public."[5] And yet these plain words were obviously long ignored, because what many authors took for a verified fact actually contained a central postulate on the function of the readymade: the fact of its exhibition was part of the essence of the readymade—and thus a readymade that had not been exhibited would have been inconceivable. If we took

2 For a compilation of the many authors who hold this view, see: Daniels, *Duchamp und die anderen*, pp. 166 and 325f. See also in detail: Blunck, *Duchamps Readymade*.

3 See for example George Dickie, *Aesthetics*, New York 1971, p. 102f.

4 Interview Tomkins, 1964, p. 26.

5 Anon., "Artist Marcel Duchamp visits U-classes, exhibits at Walker," *Minnesota Daily*, October 22, 1965.

away its confrontation with an art context, it would remain a simple object. The two examples shown here (p. 98) stand for countless others. The readymades are imagined to be exhibited "As early as 1915 ... as works of art" (Phaidon Encyclopedia 1978). The importance of the urinal is highlighted by the (fake) news that it was "signed" and "put on display in 1917" (BBC News 2004) —while it originally was neither displayed in public nor signed (at least with Duchamp's name). Alfred Stieglitz's subtle black and white photograph of the "*Fountain*" on a pedestal may have had its part in creating this misunderstanding, yet it shows a situation staged for the photographing of the object, the truth is it was never exhibited this way.

A more thorough examination of the readymades' reception history shows that at the time of their original creation (and long after) they were not exhibited at all. In the period between 1914 and 1917, Duchamp only undertook the two tests described above: during their first exhibition at the Bourgeois Gallery in 1916 the objects went unnoticed, while the second tryout—arranged to gain a much larger potential publicity—ended with the rejection of the urinal submitted to the "Independents," so that it did not enter the exhibition.

Not a single one of the pure readymades listed in the first part of this text were exhibited during those years, in the sense that it would have found recognition as a readymade created by Duchamp. Also, we find no trace of the term readymade in the art literature of the time. Only after the reception of the readymade concept had already begun in the sphere of Surrealism did

Duchamp first show a replica of the long lost Bottle Dryer within that context, in 1936 at the *Exposition Surréaliste d'Objets* in the Charles Ratton gallery in Paris.[6]

WHY READYMADES IN THE STUDIO?

So where were the readymades if they were not being exhibited? The simple answer is: after Duchamp had selected them, the readymades were in his studio. This may sound banal, but it is not self-evident, since it is typical that the studio is the primary place for artistic production. The imposing building in which Duchamp had his New York studio was designed in 1903 especially for artists and architects and today it still goes by the name of "The Atelier."[7] And yet since the readymades, as finished goods, were not actually produced by Duchamp, he could have shipped them directly from the department store to the exhibition space—that is, if it

6 See in more detail: Daniels, *Duchamp und die anderen*, pp. 195–202 (chapter: "Das sukzessive Bekanntwerden der Readymades in den 30er Jahren").

7 Today real-estate agents use the famous former inhabitant to advertise the building: "Off-course [*sic*] there were a series of great artists who lived / worked inside its walls the most enduring being Dadaist and Surrealist Marcel Duchamp who lived there between 1915 to 1921." (http://streeteasy.com/building/the-atelier).

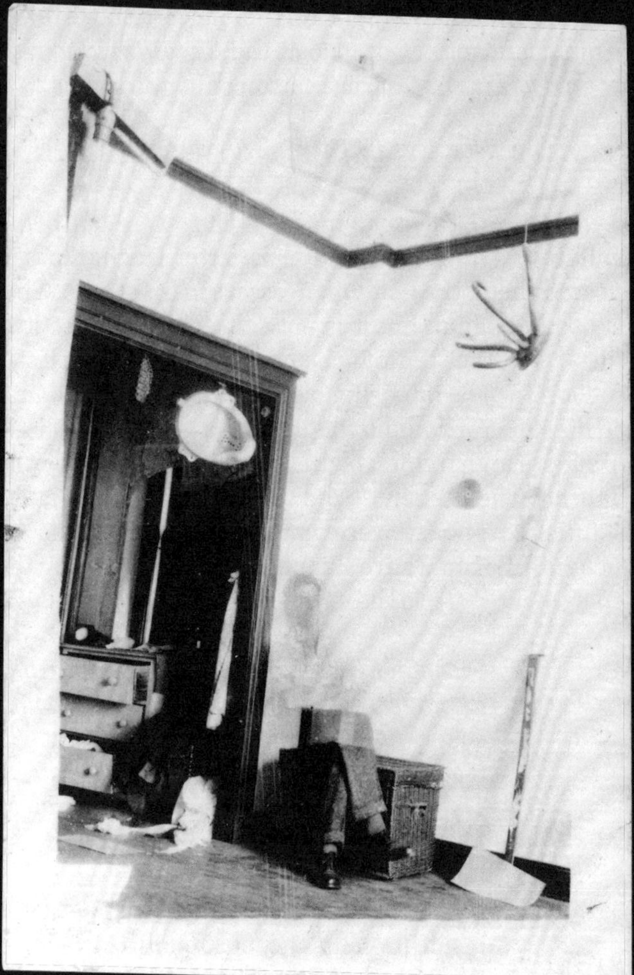

Photograph of Marcel Duchamp's studio, ca. 1917–18, attributed to Henri-Pierre Roché

had really been his main objective to publicly exhibit utility objects in an art context.

In Henri-Pierre Roché's photographs of the studio in 33 West 67th Street, made around 1917, 1918, we see how Duchamp installed the readymades within the space. It seems that his contemporaries could hardly tell if they were single works or an ensemble of objects. For example, Duchamp's friend, the art collector Katherine Dreier, wrote in a letter from 1917 to the artist: "The only 'readymades' I saw were groups which are extremely original in their handling. I did not know that you had conceived of single objects."[8] When journalist Nixola Greeley-Smith interviewed Duchamp with two artist friends who had just arrived from Paris in 1916, she described the large, shiny shovel hanging from the ceiling, which obviously had never been used and that attracted her fascinated eye immediately on entering the studio.[9] And yet during the course of their charming conversation nobody refers to the fact that this might be an actual work by Duchamp. Also the term ready-

8 The letter is part of Dreier's argument for the rejection of "*Fountain*" (letter from April 13, 1917, Katherine S. Dreier Papers, Beinecke Rare Book & Manuscript Library, Yale University).

9 Nixola Greeley-Smith, "Cubist Depicts Love in Brass and Glass," *The Evening World*, April 4, 1916, reprinted in: Rudolf E. Kuenzli (ed.), *New York Dada*, New York 1986, pp. 135–137.

made is never once mentioned, while Jean Crotti comments in some detail on the aesthetic qualities of a pair of muddy galoshes in the corner of the studio.

We will have to discuss to what extent the readymades in Duchamp's studio were single pieces, or situative and variable constellations of objects within the space. We can hardly answer this from a study of the scarce contemporary sources, even if the evidence suggests that we can understand Duchamp's studio as a "laboratory of perception," in Herbert Molderings' words.[10] Even if the studio at that time opened its doors to the occasional visitor, it did not offer a semi-public platform for the reception of the readymades. Instead it appears that Duchamp initially created the readymades—as Lars Blunck has put it—"for himself," and not for an audience.[11] In New York he implemented the program already sketched out in the note he wrote in Paris 1913: "Can one make works which are not works of 'art'?"[12]

10 Herbert Molderings, "It Is Not the Objects That Count, but the Experiments: Marcel Duchamp's New York Studio as a Laboratory of Perception," in: *Re-Object: Marcel Duchamp, Damien Hirst, Jeff Koons, Gerhard Merz*, ed. by Eckhard Schneider, Kunsthaus Bregenz 2007, pp. 146–154.

11 Lars Blunck at the conference *100 Jahre Readymade: How to make a readymade?*, Staatliche Kunsthalle Karlsruhe, January 16, 2016.

12 Sanouillet and Peterson, *The Essential*

Because the moment the readymades would be made public, that much Duchamp suspected, they would automatically become "art," no matter if he wanted to or not.

Twenty years later, when he decided to finally publicize a comprehensive selection of the readymades—most of which in the meantime had been lost—in *Boîte-en-valise*, Duchamp resorted to the photos of his New York studio. After some deliberation, he deleted the word "studio" from the caption, which had already been printed, so in the end only the address and the date were left: "33 West 67th. New-York (1917–18)."[13]

Thus at the time of their creation, the readymades could be seen neither in exhibitions nor in a traditional artist's studio as a *work in progress*, instead they existed almost exclusively as part of Duchamp's very personal conceptual universe.

If they had remained as this "personal experiment" within the artist's "laboratory of perception," then nobody would still talk about the readymades today. When Duchamp moved from New York to Buenos Aires in 1918, he left few traces of these activities. Crucially, the relevance of the readymade for art history today is based on its later reception. The initial impulse for that reception, though, was sparked by nobody but Duchamp himself, who later positioned the readymades on the stage of the art world. This included presenting newly selected replicas of lost objects in exhibitions as well as

Writings of Marcel Duchamp, p. 74.

13 Ecke Bonk, *Marcel Duchamp: Box in a Valise*, New York 1989, p. 239.

the complex reconstruction of his activities with the help of reproductions and remakes in the period between 1936 and 1964—two parallel strategies we will examine closer in the following.

WHEN (AND IN WHAT MANNER) WERE THE READYMADES EXHIBITED?

The *Bottle Dryer*, bought in Paris in 1914 and later went missing, had its first public appearance in the form of a replica shown at the *Exposition Surréaliste d'Objets*, Galerie Charles Ratton, Paris 1936. This first publicly relevant exhibition of a readymade immediately meant a reinterpretation of an object that had remained invisible so far. Here it was embedded in a suggestive constellation including fetish objects from New Guinea and mathematical instruments from the Institut Henri Poincaré. Directly below, representing Surrealist objects, stood Meret Oppenheim's recently created "*Le Déjeuner en fourrure*," the so called fur cup.

This presentation illustrates the prehistory that the Surrealists were attempting to claim in their relatively belated enthusiasm for *objets trouvés*. Duchamp was fully aware that this constellation of objects had few things in common with his own quest for aesthetic indifference. In a later interview he commented: "My readymades have nothing to do with the *objet trouvé* because the so-called 'found object' is completely directed by personal taste. Personal taste decides that this is a beautiful object and is unique."[14]

14 Interview Kuh, 1961, p. 90.

At the time of this exhibition, a text containing a first overview of Duchamp's work for a wide audience was published in a French art magazine. The author was Gabrièle Buffet-Picabia, a close friend of Duchamp's, she explained the principle of the readymade as a conceptual approach that could not be reduced to concrete objects: "Pushed to the extreme, this rejecting leads to the very negation of achievement. It is useless to beget the work in any special material, to give it any finite form, and trademark, to recreate for the senses the subject conceived in the spirit. The visual world becomes a dictio-nary of subjects which [the artist] isolates and qualifies according to his choice; representation and interpretation are now only useless and old-fashioned finery; the privilege he confers by this differentiation is sufficient, and in this is the principle of the *readymade*."[15]

The text was accompanied by the full-page illustration of a replica of the *Bottle Dryer*, photographed by Man Ray especially for the occasion. By the end of 1936 the *Bottle Dryer*, in the form of this photograph, would be presented at the Museum of Modern Art in New York as part of the exhibition *Fantastic Art, Dada, Surrealism*. Two decades after the failed dedication as a "readymade at a distance" the Bottle Dryer enters the public domain on three prominent venues in three different formats.

15 Gabrièle Buffet-Picabia, "Cœurs volants," in: *Cahiers d'Art*, nos. 1–2, 1936, p. 38f. English translation in: View. *The Modern Magazine*, p. 15.

While the rediscovery of the readymade was taking place in 1936—and with it also its reinvention—a double strategy took shape: on the one hand replicas were exhibited in changing constellations, on the other a reinterpretation was offered through published reproductions. As we see in Gabrièle Buffet-Picabia's text, this strategy led to an art-theoretical reception, which continues to the present day, and shows no signs of letting up a hundred years after the lost "originals."

Despite their concerted outing in Paris and New York, no immediate readymade boom conquered the art world after 1936. The next known appearance of a readymade was in 1950, when the Sidney Janis Gallery in New York exhibited "*Fountain*," followed by a second appearance at the same place three years later, as part of the Dada exhibition curated by Duchamp. On that occasion, Duchamp placed himself in the context of Dadaism, although his relations to the movement had been distant back in the day—as documented by the well-known telegram "PODE BAL" that he sent in 1921 to decline his participation in the "Salon Dada."[16]

Two things are remarkable when it comes to these first two public appearances of "*Fountain*" after 32 and 35 years respectively: in 1950, Duchamp left the choice

16 In this telegram, Duchamp uses a phonetic shorthand for the French expression *peau de balle* (skin of the testicles), meaning: "nuts to you," or, "nothing doing." Sanouillet and Peterson, *The Essential Writings of Marcel Duchamp*, p. 180.

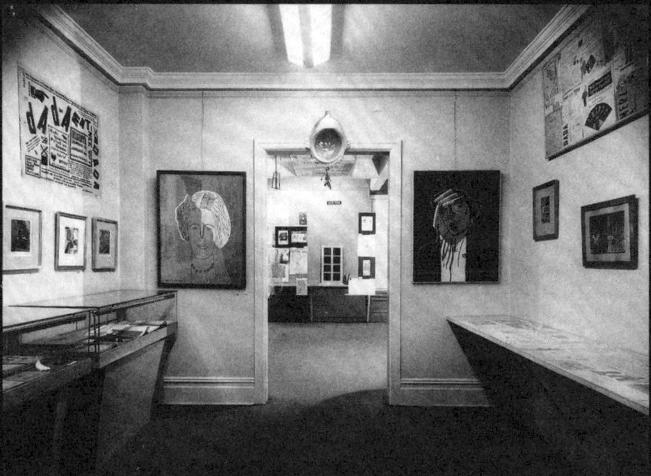

Dada, 1916–1923 *at Sidney Janis Gallery, New York 1953,* "Fountain" *over door*

of a urinal to the gallerist Sidney Janis, and in 1953 he placed the object above the doorframe of a passageway, similar to the position in Henri-Pierre Roché's photographs of Duchamp's studio.

From these cursory glances into the early public life of the readymades, we can derive the following theses:

- Any exhibition or publication of a readymade departs from the original concept of a "personal experiment."
- Exhibiting and reproducing the readymades proves to be its own form of "art," a permanent reconfiguration and reinterpretation, at least as long as Duchamp himself directs their appearances.
- Their presentation in new combinations can be understood as a reference back to the way the readymades appeared as an ensemble in the artist's studio at 33 West 67th Street.
- There is no "correct" form of presentation for the readymades at exhibitions—rather, the variability of presentation modes is appropriate to the initial idea of the readymade.[17]

17 Cf. Duchamp: "They had no absolute determination, that is, no absolutely required form of presentation." (Interview Collin 1967, p. 38.) Accordingly, a panel discussion on Marcel Duchamp's presentations of the readymades, *Before the Readymade Was Ready to Be Ready Made*, on occasion of the exhibition *Friedrich Christian Flick Collection im*

HOW WERE DUCHAMP'S READYMADES (RE-)MADE FOR PRESENTATION IN EXHIBITIONS?

The most influential presentation of the readymades was not as single replicas in an exhibition, but rather as in the context of a "musée imaginaire" (André Malraux) of ideal reproductions, or as "works of art in the age of mechanical reproduction" (Walter Benjamin).[18] At the time of their first exhibitions in 1936, Duchamp reconstructed and represented the readymades in *Boîte-en-valise* (1936–1941). This without a doubt was the "exhibition" that had the strongest impact.

With *Boîte-en-valise*, Duchamp not only gave us a first overview of his work, he also established dates and titles for his pieces that are still accepted today. The documentation of lost objects by means of historical photographs became part of his varied strategies for the presentation of the readymades. Partly these images were retouched so thoroughly that we can speak of a

Hamburger Bahnhof on 2. December, 2004, with Hans M. de Wolf, Herbert Molderings, and Dieter Daniels remained without much of a result.

18 Walter Benjamin learned of Duchamp's *Boîte-en-valise* during a chance meeting in Paris one year after the publication of his essay, and he considered discussing it in another text on the topic. See: Naumann, *The Art of Making Art in the Age of Mechanical Reproduction*, p. 18.

reconstruction *after* the original photographs. In the case of the photo captioned "33 West 67th. New-York (1917–18)," Duchamp colorized the historical black and white of the studio view. In these procedures, we see less a documentation of the readymades rather than a declaration—and the coat rack titled "*Trébuchet*" becomes a readymade only by this declaration, because without that it would only be a strangely out-of-place object like the pillow on the floor beside it. The *Hat Rack* and the *Snow Shovel* likewise stand out from their surroundings because they have been retouched.[19]

Obviously the historical photographs had not been made to document single objects, but to give an overall impression of the room and the unusual constellation of things within. Again, the situative aspect of the readymades comes to the fore, which Duchamp still tried to preserve in the first exhibitions of the exact replicas.

For the three small models of readymades in *Boîte-en-valise*, which were prominently positioned and produced with extreme care, Duchamp developed a new type of constellation. The objects were no longer occupying a space in a situative arrangement, as they were in his New York studio during 1916–17, instead they were related to the *Large Glass*. Thus the urinal corresponds to the hollow shapes of the bachelors in the lower half of the glass; the typewriter cover (which according to Duchamp should be associated with a woman's skirt) is placed in the middle, where the bachelors meet the bride;

19 See the detailed study by Bonk, *Box in a Valise*, pp. 234f and 239f.

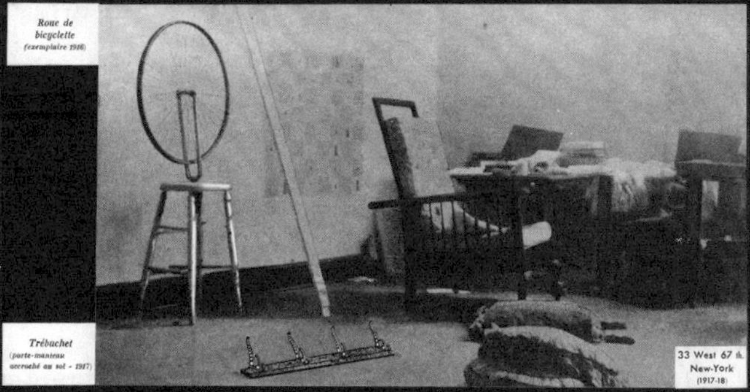

33 West 67th. New-York *(1917–18) from* Boîte-en-valise.

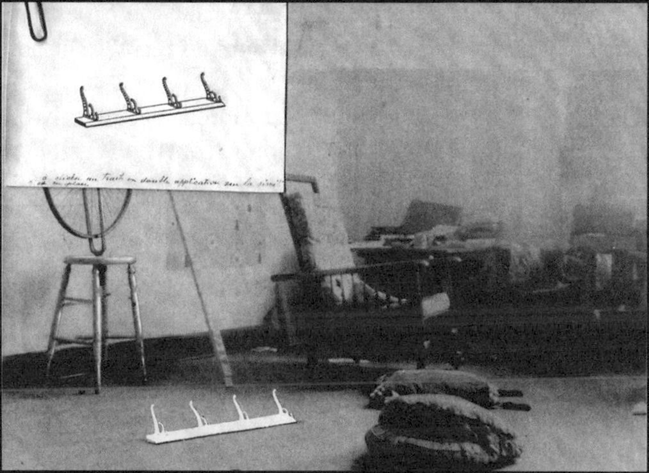

Intermediate stages in the preparation of a historical photograph for Boîte-en-valise.

the air-filled glass ampoule is analogous to the bride's suspended cloud hovering in the upper half. Later Duchamp would transfer this constellation into the context of a museum exhibition, with replicas of the three readymades in their original size.[20] Here again we see Duchamp's playful and variable approach to exhibition forms, a far cry from the standardized presentation of the readymades as objects on a pedestal that can be seen in many museums.

Like the later edition of multiples, the three miniaturized readymade remakes reveal very different strategies of reconstruction: the original object was at hand as a model for "*Air de Paris*," Alfred Stieglitz's photograph of the lost original served as a point of reference for "*Fountain*," while no point of reference existed for "... *Pliant ... de Voyage*" apart from the artist's own memory. With his meticulous documentation and reconstruction of the readymades, Duchamp paved the way for their future reception, which is based almost exclusively on *Boîte-en-valise* and the artist's notes from the *Green Box*.

20 At Duchamp's first museum retrospective, *By or of Marcel Duchamp or Rrose Sélavy*, curated by Walter Hopps at the Pasadena Art Museum in 1963 (now called Norton Simon Museum). The exhibition presented the readymade remakes fabricated by Ulf Linde for the Duchamp exhibition at Galerie Burén in Stockholm, 1963.

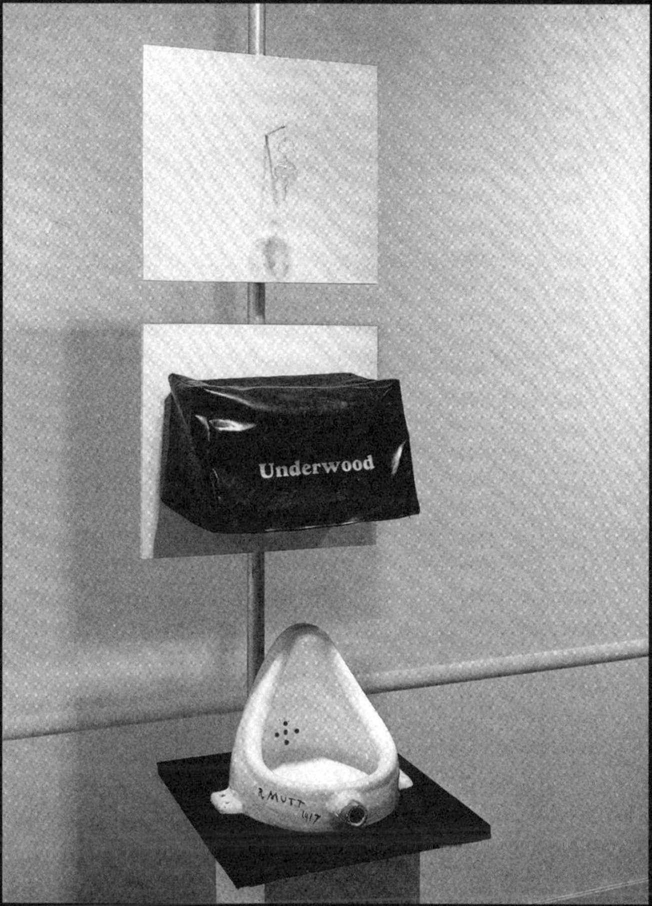

Three readymade remakes (by Ulf Linde) in Duchamp's first museum retrospective, Pasadena Museum of Art, October 8–November 3, 1963.

THE SELF-APPROPRIATION OF DUCHAMP: REMAKES AS ORIGINALS

In interviews and statements of the 1960s, Duchamp emphasized that the readymades were not to be seen as originals, but could at any time be replaced by replicas: "Another aspect of the 'Readymade' is its lack of uniqueness... The replica of a 'Readymade' delivering the same message; in fact nearly every one of the 'Readymades' existing today is not an original in the conventional sense."[21]

This statement can only be applied to pure, unmodified readymades. *A readymade rectifié*—such as the postcard with a reproduction of the Mona Lisa, to which Duchamp added a thin moustache, a small pointed beard, and the title "*L.H.O.O.Q.*"—definitely carries the status of an original. This status was even authenticated by Duchamp in 1944, when he added a notarial certification on the back: "This is to certify / that this is the original / 'ready made' L.H.O.O.Q. / Paris 1919 / Marcel Duchamp / New York 1944."[22] Aesthetically, the subtly drawn beard of the original from 1919 is very different from the edition produced in 1965, where Duchamp sketched in the beard 38 times, one for each copy of the edition.

For the pure, unmodified readymade, the status of an original would be meaningless. It could easily be

21 Marcel Duchamp, "Apropos of Readymades" (see p. 46 in this book)
22 Schwarz, *Complete Works*, № 369.

replaced by an equivalent replica (as long as Duchamp added the inscription). There are basically two possibilities of creating such a replica: one can either buy a similar "ready-made" product and accept the range of variations within a palette of the same product, or one can produce from raw material an object as close as possible to the original.

The fundamental difference between the simple selection of an object and the manual fabrication of a remake has hardly been noticed among Duchamp scholars. For example, of the *Bottle Dryer's* seven replicas listed in Duchamp's *Complete Works*, five have been newly bought and two have been recreated. Duchamp signed *Bottle Dryers* whose forms varied considerably in 1921, 1936, 1960, 1961, and 1963. Ulf Linde was the first to replicate a single copy of the *Bottle Dryer* in 1963 for the Duchamp exhibition at the Gallery Burén in Stockholm. In 1964 followed the edition of multiples produced by Galleria Schwarz.[23]

This edition of "14 Readymades" from 1964 ended Duchamp's practice of freely signing any bottle dryer or urinal, since a contract with Galleria Schwarz obliged

23 Ibid., № 306. Ulf Linde's hand-made single replicas of the readymades served as models for the edition of multiples produced by Galleria Schwarz. See the extensive research on Linde's readymade remakes by Paul B. Franklin "Exposing Duchamp in Sweden," in *Étant donné* № 11, Paris 2016, pp. 94–141.

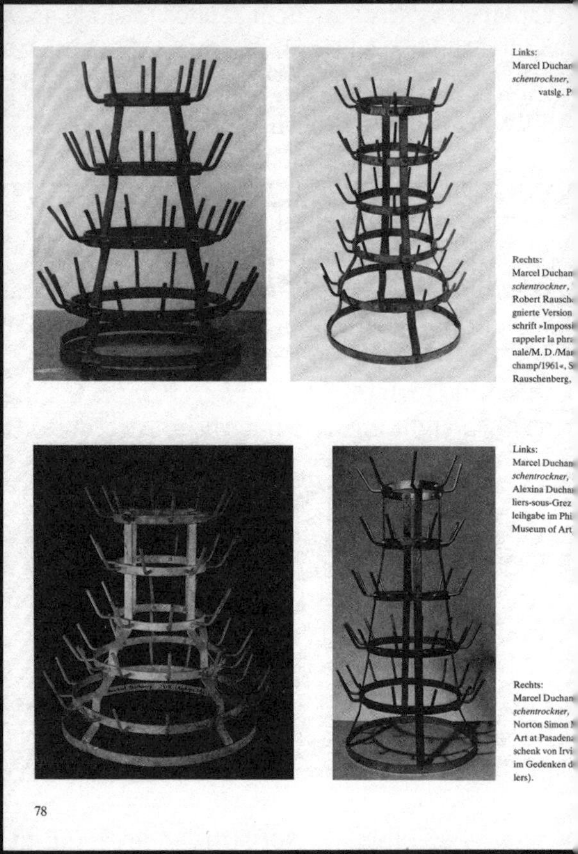

Different versions of the Bottlerack *Spread from the catalog: Dieter Daniels and Alfred M. Fischer,* Übrigens sterben immer die anderen: Marcel Duchamp und die Avantgarde seit 1950, *Museum Ludwig, Cologne 1988, pp. 78–79. (see also p. 153f in this book for details)*

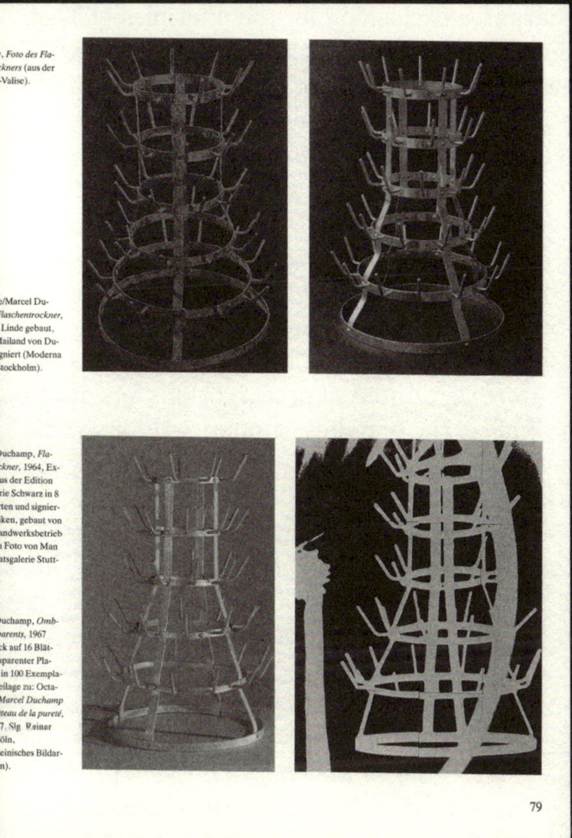

Left: various found "ready-made" Bottle Dryers *signed by Marcel Duchamp from 1921–63*

Right: Photo by Man Ray for Boîte-en-valise *(1936) and the subsequent replica models built after this photo by Ulf Linde and Arturo Schwarz*

him to guarantee exclusivity for the multiples.[24] Their standardized shape, which, according to Arturo Schwarz, had to match the original form, now replaced the previous variety of objects. In this way, Schwarz retroactively accorded the status of an original to the "pure" ready-mades after which the edition was modeled—a status they did not previously have in Duchamp's view. In 1964 one could easily have bought a new "ready-made" bottle dryer, and yet for the edition of multiples they were specifically produced in a small series, same as the urinal, the snow shovel, the comb, the coat rack, and the hat rack.

There were very different preconditions for the fabrication of each of the remakes, similar to the situation for *Boîte-en-valise*. The breadth of variations reached from making a copy of an existing original (comb), through reconstructions after historical photos of the missing originals (urinal, snow shovel, coat rack, hat rack), to constructions without any surviving documents for the original (bottle dryer, typewriter cover).[25]

24 See Duchamp's letter from 1964 in: Naumann, *The Art of Making Art in the Age of Mechanical Reproduction*, p. 245.

25 In the first edition of Arturo Schwarz's *Collected Works* from 1969, we still find the following information for several of the objects that were not documented in photographs before they became part of the edition of multiples in 1964: "First full scale-replicas issued under the direct supervision of Duchamp on the basis of a blueprint derived from photos of the lost

Schwarz did not address this heterogeneous state of the record, but had vertical sections and cross-sections for all of the "14 Readymades" drawn by draftmans from which the multiples were then produced.[26] In contrast to the individualization of the readymade in *Boîte-en-valise*, we can speak of a homogenization of the objects' different appearances in the "14 Readymades."

In the actual fabrication of these objects, the paradox of a remake after a model which had been declared an original post facto became even stronger. How could a three-dimensional remake of the urinal be produced after Alfred Stieglitz's frontal shot from 1917, without knowing what the object looked like in profile? What basis could there be for objects where no photo of the original had survived, e.g. for the typewriter cover "... *Pliant ... de Voyage*" or the *Bottle Dryer*? In fact, the multiple of the *Bottle Dryer* was produced after Man Ray's photo of

original" (№ 219, *Bottle Dryer*; № 240, *Traveler's Folding Item*). This is later corrected, so that in the edition of 1997 we read under № 342, Traveler's Folding Item: "No photograph of the original Readymade exists." And on the corresponding multiple: "Produced under the artist's supervision after the *Boîte-en-valise* reproduction." See for details: Martha Buskirk, *The Contingent Object of Contemporary Art*, Cambridge and London 2003, p. 70.

26 Schwarz, *Complete Works*, nos. 595–598 and 601–605.

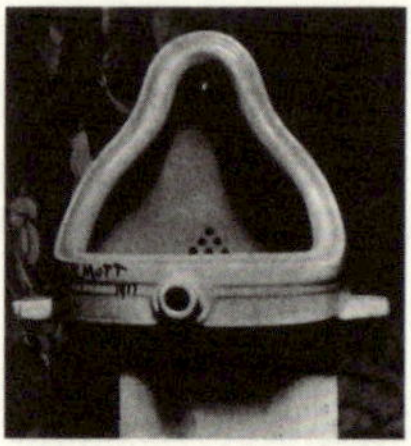

original

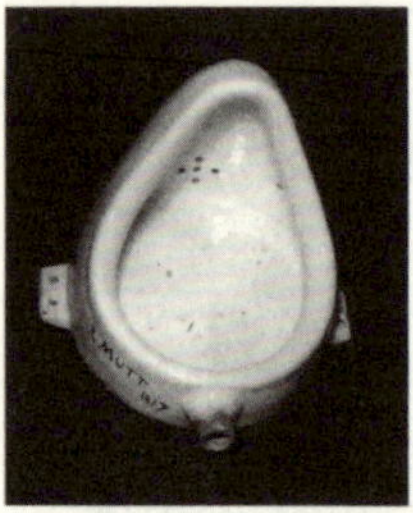

a

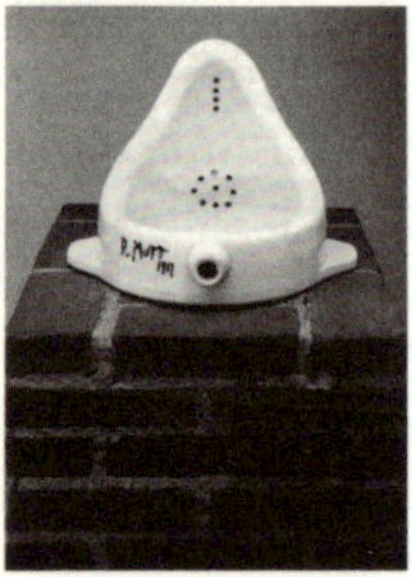

c

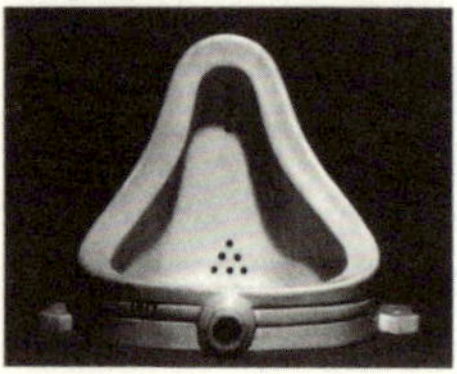

d

tion as though it were a marble Aphrodite, Arensberg turned and in his quiet voice tendered his resignation from the Society of Independent Artists."[1]

The pseudonym Duchamp adopted was meant to enforce the value of the choice: "Mutt comes from Mott Works, the name of a large sanitary equipment manufacturer. But Mott was too close so I altered it to Mutt, after the daily cartoon strip 'Mutt and Jeff' which appeared at the time, and with which everyone was familiar. Thus, from the start, there was an interplay of Mutt: a fat little funny man, and Jeff: a tall, thin man . . . I wanted any old name. And I added Richard [French slang for moneybags]. That's not a bad name for a *pissotiere*. Get it? The opposite of poverty. But not even that much, just R. MUTT."[2]

Duchamp's friend Beatrice Wood was an observer of the event: "I was also present at the dispute about the Urinal upside-down, between Arensberg and Bellows, or it may have been Rockwell Kent. Bellows said it could not be accepted. Arensberg insisted [that] the sender had given six dollars and that it had to be. . . . I published one issue of *The Blind Man* with the picture of the Urinal, because Marcel and Roché, being under the French Government, felt it better for their names not to appear. We were going to put it on sale, but when my father saw the mountains of magazines in the front hall of our correct and fashionable apartment, he opened the package, was horrified that his sweet little daughter had lent her name to such a horrible collection of ideas. I thereupon got in touch with Frank Crowninshield, editor of *Vanity Fair*, said that my father was an honest, bon bourgeois, and if he reacted so violently to the whole affair, maybe it would shock other good citizens, and that thereby it might be unwise to send it through the mails. Crowninshield and I reread the proofs, decided that since some well-known names were connected with it, it would be better to protect them from criticism. *The Blind Man* was given out by hand to friends, art collectors and galleries."[3]

The issue of *The Blind Man* to which Beatrice Wood refers carried an unsigned editorial called "The Richard Mutt Case," which Duchamp was believed to have written: "They say any artist paying six dollars may exhibit. Mr. Richard Mutt sent in a fountain. Without discussion this article disappeared and never was exhibited. What were the

Different versions of the "Fountain," *as published in: Arturo Schwarz,* The Complete Works of Marcel Duchamp, *New York 2000*

the replica from 1936 (and in the meantime also lost), which Duchamp already had used for *Boîte-en-valise*.

Let us return to our earlier question: Have you ever seen a readymade? If you can remember where and when, in all probability you will find that it was one of the remakes, a multiple from the "14 Readymades" of 1964. So when we encounter one of these multiples of the "*Fountain*" or the *Bottle Dryer* in an exhibition today, what do we actually see?

In the case of "*Fountain*": we see the three-dimensional reconstruction of a lost urinal, *after* the photograph by Alfred Stieglitz from 1917, *after* the section drawings that a technical draftsman based on this photo, cast in porcelain from these drawings by a manufacturer of sanitary goods in 1964.

In the case of the *Bottle Dryer*: we see the three-dimensional reconstruction of a lost object that has left no photographical record, *after* an idea by Duchamp from 1914, *after* a replica of this idea from 1936, *after* the photograph of this replica by Man Ray from that same year, and *after* section drawings that a technical draftsman based on this photo, which was then produced from these drawings by Italian craftsmen in 1964.

But maybe our question—have you ever seen a readymade?—has only led us astray. Because it presupposes that the traditional idea of the personal, authentic experience of an artwork still remains significant. Yet this is exactly denied by Duchamp. When asked by Philippe Collin how a readymade should be looked at, he answered: "Ultimately, it should not be looked at.

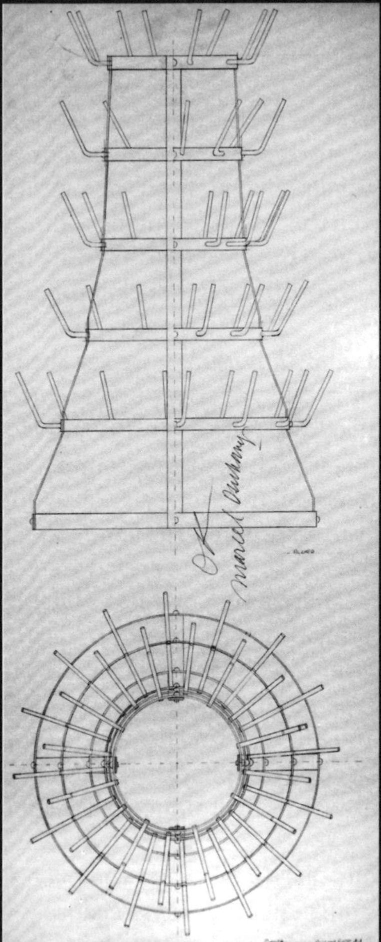

Blueprint for the replica multiple of Bottle Dryer, *1964, signed "OK / Marcel Duchamp," Museu Coleção Berardo, Lisbon*

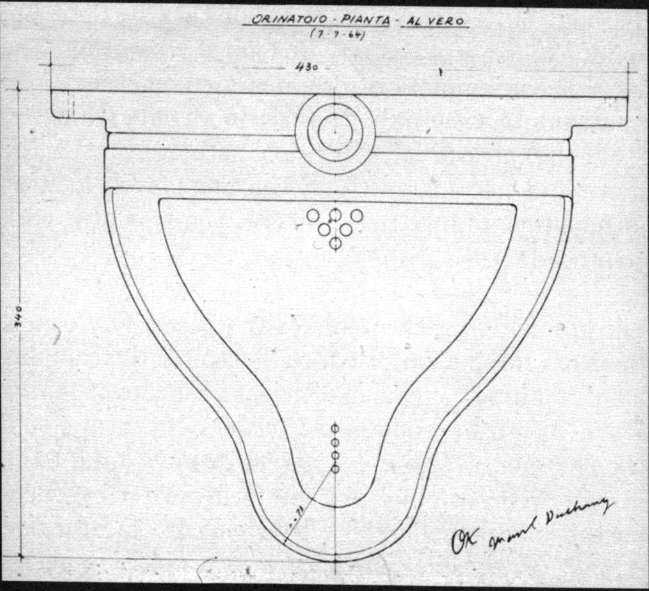

Blueprint for the replica multiple of Fountain, *1964, signed "OK / Marcel Duchamp," BIJI Collection, Tokyo*

Through our eyes we get the notion that it exists. But we don't look at it the way we look at a painting. The idea of contemplation disappears completely."[27] In another interview, he had an even more radical answer: "Take the bottle dryer, which does not carry bottles anymore and becomes a thing you don't even look at, although you know that it exists, you look at it with your head turned..." [28]

The production of the remakes also raises subtle questions of reproducibility, which illustrates the complexity of "making" a readymade: does a remake of "*Air de Paris*" have to be produced in Paris?[29] What form should the threads of "*Trois Stoppages Étalon*" take—the same as in the original, or a new form created by following the same procedure?[30] What should be placed inside "*À Bruit secret*," since the concept of the work demanded

27 Interview Collin 1967, pp. 37f.

28 Alain Jouffroy, *Une révolution du regard. A propos de quelques peintres et sculpteurs contemporains*, Paris 1964, p. 119.

29 The glass ampoules were manufactured in Paris (see Schwarz, *Complete Works*, p. 48). Bill Copley demanded an assurance to that effect from Schwarz before buying a copy (see Naumann, *The Art of Making Art in the Age of Mechanical Reproduction*, pp. 249 and 254).

30 The threads of the multiples follow the same shape as those of the original from 1913–14.

that Walter Conrad Arensberg was the only person to know what created the rattling noises inside it? And what seems to be even more mysterious: Why does the multiple of the Comb have two teeth less than the original preserved in the Philadelphia Museum of Art? [31]

In the appropriation art of the 1980s, we find similarly convoluted stages of authorship. Here we might think of the exhibition *Sherrie Levine after Walker Evans* (New York 1981), in which Levine first showed her re-photographs of photos by Walker Evans. Duchamp's remakes were similarly based on photos of the bottle dryer or the urinal by Man Ray or Alfred Stieglitz respectively. In the end, Duchamp appropriated his *own* work half a century later.

Arturo Schwarz advertised the edition of multiples as the definitive version of the readymades, authenticated by the artist himself. But from the perspective of appropriation art, we could see them as a completely new type of work: the readymades *as* multiples are Duchamp *after* Duchamp. They are an act of self-appropriation unique at the time (whose possible function as a model for 1980s appropriation art has hardly been studied yet).

31 Thomas Girst proposes to link these slight differences to Duchamp's concept of the inframince "in the way that they probe the infinitesimal difference between objects that look alike." Thomas Girst, *The Duchamp Dictionary*, London 2014, p. 65.

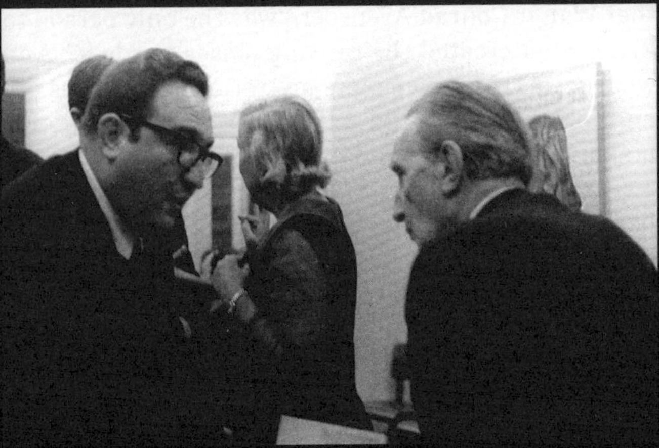

Marcel Duchamp and Arturo Schwarz at the finissage of Marcel Duchamp, même, *Kestnergesellschaft, Hanover, September 28, 1965. (photograph by Umbo).*

EXHIBITING REMAKES OF READYMADES

The remakes of the "14 Readymades" led to a substantial presence in exhibitions and museum collections, which continues to this day. This started with an international tour of five stations in Europe and others in the U.S. from 1964–1965. The readymades were shown in different contexts, sometimes in monographic Duchamp exhibitions, sometimes in combination with other artistic positions of classical modernism.[32]

EXHIBITIONS OF THE "14 READYMADES" IN VARIOUS CONTEXTS

- *Omaggio a Marcel Duchamp*, Galleria Schwarz, Milan, June 5 to September 30, 1964. (see also p. 38f in this book for details)

Further stations:

- *Marcel Duchamp, Wassily Kandinsky, Kazimir Malevich, Josef Albers, Tom Doyle*, Kunsthalle Bern, October to November, 1964
- Marcel Duchamp, Gimpel Fils, London, December 1964 to January 1965

32 In the publication accompanying the exhibition, Arturo Schwarz elaborates a categorization for the different types of readymades. He updates André Breton's definition, linking it to the concept of "appropriation" of Pierre Restany. Walter Hopps, Ulf Linde, Arturo Schwarz, Marcel Duchamp: Ready-mades, etc., 1913–1964, Galleria Schwarz, Milan 1964, p. 24.

- *Marcel Duchamp: Schilderijen, tekeningen, ready-mades*, Haags Gemeentemuseum, Den Haag, February to March 1965, and Stedelijk van Abbemuseum, Eindhoven, March to May 1965
- *Marcel Duchamp*, Museum Haus Lange, Krefeld, July 1965
- *Marcel Duchamp, même*, Kestnergesellschaft, Hanover, September 1965

Meanwhile in the U.S.:
- *Not Seen and / or Less Seen of / by Marcel Duchamp / Rrose Selavy* 1904–64, Cordier & Ekstrom, Inc., New York, January to February 1965

Further stations:
- Museum of Fine Arts, Houston, February to March 1965
- Baltimore Museum of Art, May to June 1965
- Rose Art Museum, Brandeis University, Waltham, MA, July to August 1965
- Milwaukee Art Center, September to October 1965
- Walker Art Center, Minneapolis, October to November 1965

Subsequently traveling, in 1967 / 68, to ten museums and art galleries throughout Australia and New Zealand in reduced form under the title *Marcel Duchamp: The Mary Sisler Collection*, 78 Works 1904–1963.

With the worldwide launch of Duchamp's multiples—which was also a strategically astute move within the art market—the readymades entered the canon of modernism. As the multiples of the "14 Readymades" were

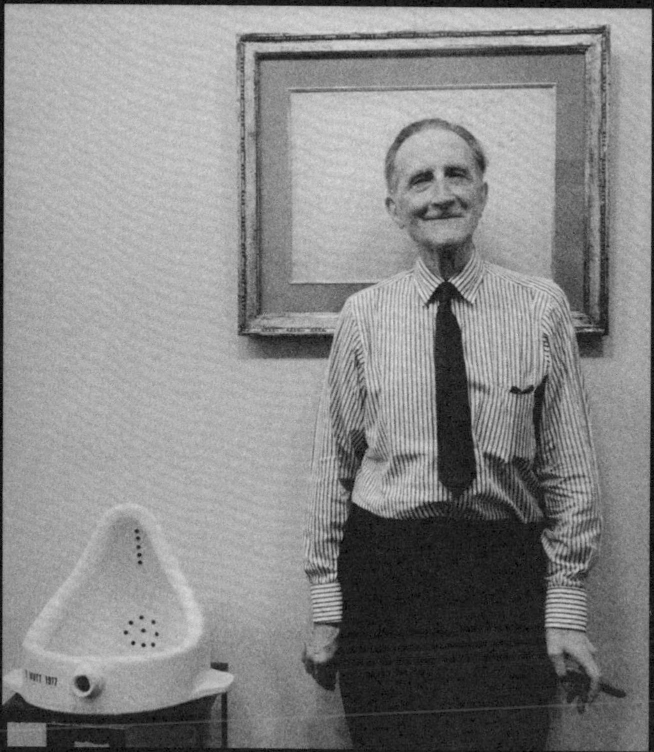

Marcel Duchamp and the "Fountain" *replica by Ulf Linde at* Omaggio a Marcel Duchamp, *Galleria Schwarz, Milan, June 5 to September 30, 1964 (photograph by Ugo Mulas)*

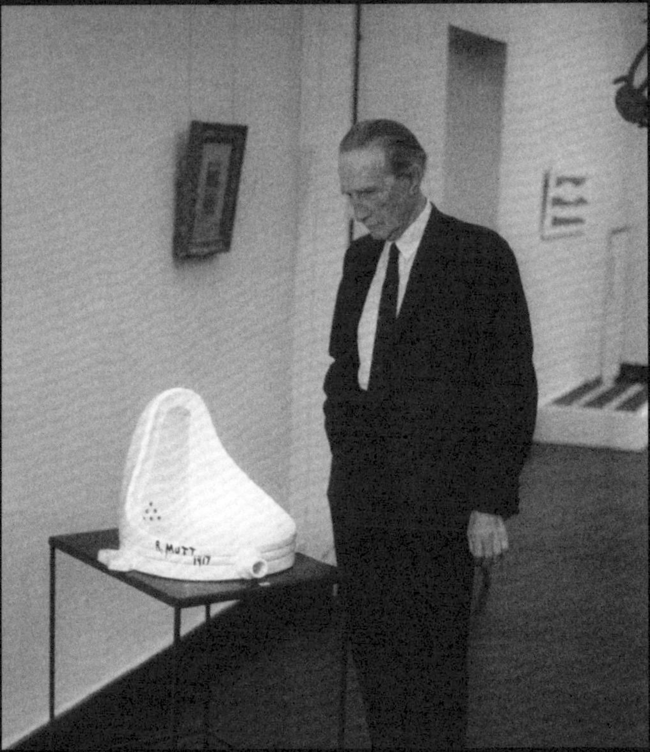

Marcel Duchamp and the "Fountain" *multiple at* Marcel Duchamp, même, *Kestnergesellschaft, Hanover, September 28, 1965 (photograph by Umbo).*

produced in editions of eight copies plus two artist copies as well as two exhibition copies each, all in all we now have the very considerable number of 168 objects still crowding the museums.

These limited remakes of everyday objects were never made for use; they were always solely objects to be looked at in exhibitions. Only in the form of their remakes did the readymades become part of the art market. Maybe we could even say that the art market was the true producer of these remakes. The basic principle of these objects, which had been selected, isolated, and withdrawn from their original practical use by Duchamp between 1914 and 1917, was now turned from its head to its feet. It appears that the readymades had to be (re-)manufactured first, before they could be exhibited. Only as remakes did they become exhibits in the traditional sense.

Thus Duchamp's "self-appropriation" leads into a perfectly circular self-contradiction, which the artist in an interview serenely declared to be part of a new artistic approach: "There is an absolute contradiction, but that is what is enjoyable, isn't it? Bringing in the idea of contradiction, the notion of contradiction, which is something that has never really been used, you see?"[33]

33 Interview Collin, 1967

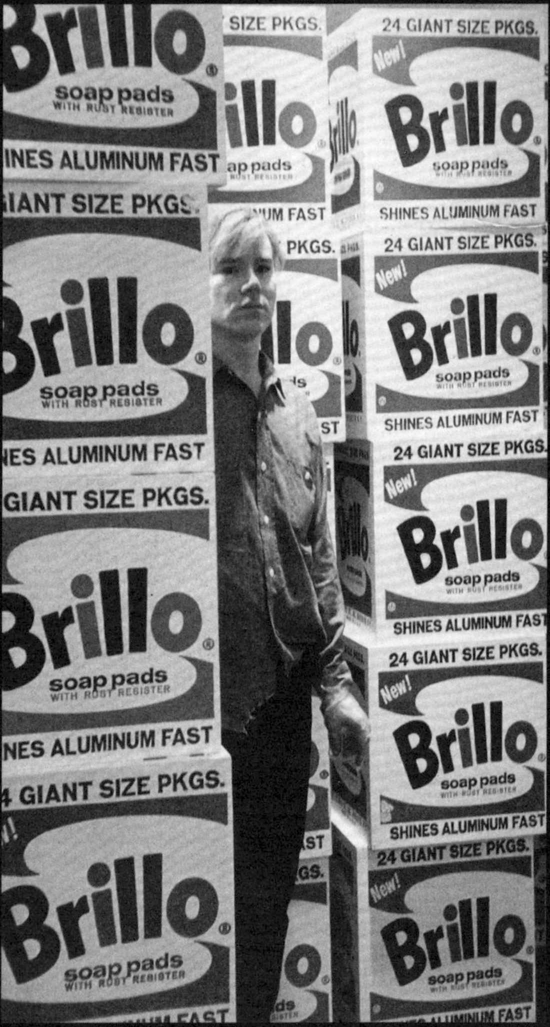

Andy Warhol and his Brillo Boxes, *Stable Gallery, New York, April 1964.*

DUCHAMP AND WARHOL:

Post-readymade remakes mark the second half of the "Readymade Century"

The readymade remakes mark the beginning of the second half of the "Readymade Century." Duchamp deliberately chose 1964 as a historical date: he commemorated the 50-year anniversary of his selection of the *Bottle Dryer* in 1914.[34] But it is also in another respect that we can see the year 1964 as a turning point from the readymade to the post-readymade. It is the year in which Andy Warhol first presented his *Brillo Boxes*—hundreds of them filled the exhibition space at their premiere in the Stable Gallery, stacked like in a supermarket.

Comparing Warhol's *Brillo Boxes* to Duchamp's readymades has become commonplace in art theory due to the pertinent writings of Arthur C. Danto. An encounter with the *Brillo Boxes* in 1964 became the initial spark for Danto's decade-long work on a nonontological art theory.[35] His analysis is often criticized because it treats

34 Schwarz, *Complete Works*, p. 48.

35 Danto proceeds from the fact "that the almost laughable inapplicability of philosophical definitions of art to art itself has been explained, by the few who perceived the inapplicability as a problem, as stemming from the indefinability

Warhol's boxes as if they were readymades, while in actual fact they are artifacts produced for the occasion.[36] At the same time, both Danto and his critics ignore the much more far-reaching parallel between the *Brillo Boxes* and Duchamp's multiples of the readymades from the same year: Warhol's silkscreened wooden boxes, which look exactly like cartons for scouring pads, are likewise multiples of remakes of consumer goods. Aside from the size of the edition, the only difference is that Duchamp's multiple remakes were produced from the same material as their models, so they are even closer to utility objects. We cannot pack anything into Warhol's remakes of Brillo boxes, while we can indeed shovel snow with the remake of a snow shovel.

Regarding their manner of presentation, the situation is the opposite: the stacks of hundreds of *Brillo Boxes* at Stable Gallery were presented as if they were real, "ready-made" cartons. Thus Warhol underlined

of art." (Arthur C. Danto, *The Transfiguration of the Commonplace*, Cambridge, MA, 1981, p. vii.) I am sympathetic to Danto's theory especially since he admits to a "philosophical intoxication" prompted by his encounter with Warhol's *Brillo Boxes* in 1964, which still had its effect when he wrote this text published in 1981 (ibid., p. vi), and would continue to inspire his investigations up to his last book, *What Art Is*, New Haven 2013.

36 Juliane Rebentisch, *Theorien der Gegenwartskunst*, Hamburg 2013, p. 122.

both their serial manufacture in his Factory studio as well as the commodity characteristics of art as a "product." In contrast, the seriality of Duchamp's remade readymades remains invisible, especially when they are presented as single objects in specially designed displays.

(EXCURSUS)

One of the earliest presentations of the readymade multiples took place in the noble, but clearly commodity-based, context of a new store for designer furniture by the manufacturer Gavina. For the opening of his flagship store in Rome (1965), Dino Gavina—still known today for his new editions of design classics from the Bauhaus, such as the Wassily chair (which Gavina had christened)—decided against a presentation of his product line. Instead, he gave the store—located in the exclusive quarters of the city's fashion strip, Via Condotti—over to the "14 Readymades," presented in elaborate displays built for the exhibition from designs by the architect Carlo Scarpa: a truly unique flagship store for readymades![37]

If the remakes of consumer goods by Warhol and Duchamp in 1964 mark the turning point from the readymade to the post-readymade, this would concern

37 See the catalog to the exhibition *Duchamp: Re-made in Italy*, Galleria nazionale d'arte moderna, October 8, 2013 to February 9, 2014, here p. 144f on Carlo Scarpa's designs of the displays for the readymades.

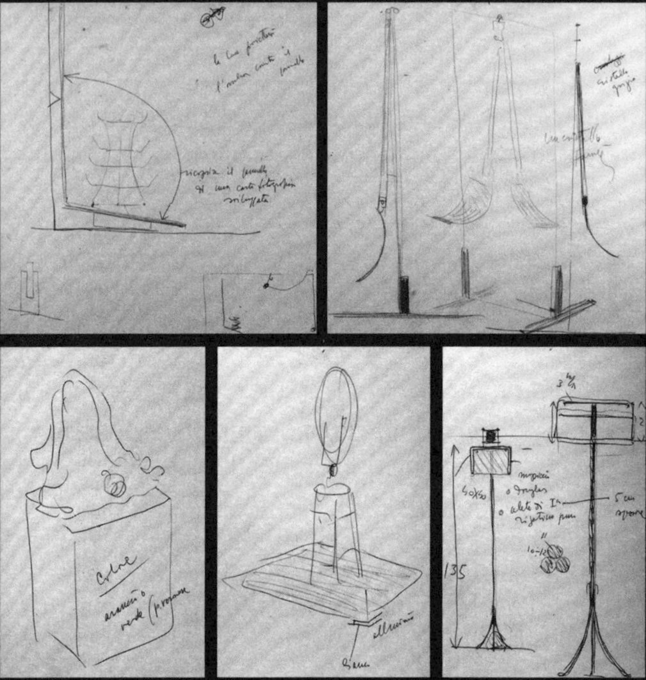

Carlo Scarpa, sketches for readymade displays, Rome 1965

not merely aspects of their fabrication, but would also have far-reaching consequences for artistic strategies in a commercial context. As Warhol's presentation of the *Brillo Boxes* at the Stable Gallery proves, the ready-made principle can be translated into an art-market strategy. In contrast, Duchamp's approach to the ready-made between 1914 and 1917 had opposed the dictates of self-repetition required by the art market: "It was really to get out of the exchangeability, I mean the monetization, one might say, of the work of art. I never intended to sell my readymades. So it was really a gesture to show that one could do something without having, in the back of your head, the idea of making money through it." This is what Duchamp stated in an interview with Calvin Tomkins, which, probably not by sheer coincidence, also took place in 1964. When Tomkins repeated his question with some incredulity, Duchamp insisted: "Never. Never did I sell them."[38]

Duchamp was completely aware that the concept of the readymades would change by selling their remade multiples. When an artist from the U.S. asked him to sign a bottle dryer he had accidentally found in the trash in 1964, Duchamp declined in view of his contract with Schwarz, and then added: "But signature or no signature, your find has the same 'metaphysical' value as any other readymade, [it] even has the advantage to have no commercial value."[39]

38 Tomkins, *The Afternoon Interviews*, p. 26.
39 Letter to Douglas Gorsline, in: Naumann, *The Art of Making Art in the Age of Mechanical Reproduction*, p. 245.

Following today's terminology, Duchamp's strategies concerning the readymade before 1917 can be seen as a critique, or—maybe more precisely—as an avoidance of the commodity character of art. In place of the commodification of art as a product, the readymades posit the product as art. With Duchamp's post-readymades from 1964, though, the readymades do become an art commodity. Thus his strategy of self-appropriation can be seen as a forebearer to the self-commodification strategies of the readymade and the 'remaking' in the work of Elaine Sturtevant, Mike Bidlo, Sherrie Levine, or Jeff Koons, with continuing success on the art market. Interestingly, Levine and Koons also started out with pure readymades and then progressed into readymade remakes—as illustrated by Koons' early appropriation of an inflatable bunny *(Inflatable Flower and Bunny [Tall White and Pink Bunny]*, 1979) versus the later replica of the same object in stainless steel (*Rabbit*, 1986). In a slightly different mode, Sherrie Levine sold 75 pairs of children's shoes she had bought "ready-made" as part of her action *Shoe Sale* in 1977. For *Two Shoes*, an edition of multiples from 1992, similar children's shoes in an edition of 135 pairs had been produced.[40] "A refined version, handmade in Italy from softest leather and suede, retraces the artist's first steps," read the blurb

40 See the interview with Sherrie Levine in: Martha Buskirk and Mignon Nixon (eds.), *The Duchamp Effect: Essays, Interviews, Round Table*, Cambridge and London 1996, p. 178.

by art magazine *Parkett*, which had commissioned the edition.[41]

In January 1965, Duchamp leaves behind his historical strategy of the readymade as an art market critique, when he signs a small reproduction of the Mona Lisa and adds the words: "rasée L.H.O.O.Q." With this gesture, Duchamp has first symbolically downgraded the original Mona Lisa to a shaved version of his own bearded Mona Lisa from 1919. Second, he admits that the beard is gone, it's all over: the readymades are now iconic artworks just like Leonardo's Mona Lisa. Third, he circumvents his contract with Arturo Schwarz, which binds him to abstain from signing any more readymades, as he is here signing an invitation card to a preview dinner, sent to about a hundred invited people free of charge. And fourth, "rasée L.H.O.O.Q." can be seen as a reference to the shaved pubis of the female figure in Duchamp's work "*Étant donnés...*," which in 1964 was almost finished but still kept a secret. And with this final gesture, seemingly inconspicuous yet elegantly coded in several ways, we leave the readymades of Marcel Duchamp, not without giving him the final word: "They look trivial, but they're not. On the contrary, they represent a much higher degree of intellectuality."[42]

41 Online at http://parkettart.com/editions/32-edition-levine.html.
42 Interview Robert 1963, p. 62.

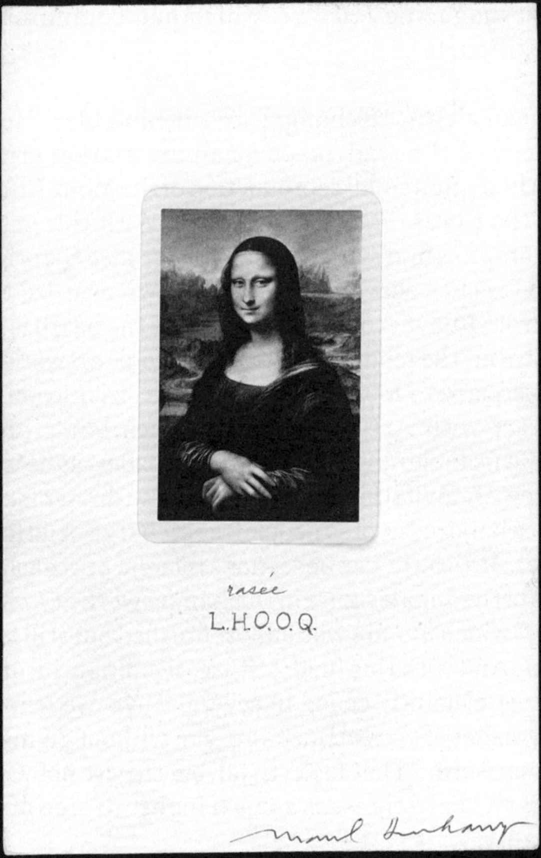

Marcel Duchamp, “rasée L.H.O.O.Q.,” *1965*

Invitation card for the preview of the exhibition Not Seen and / or Less Seen of / by Marcel Duchamp / Rrose Sélavy 1904–64, *Cordier & Ekstrom, Inc. New York, ca. 100 copies.*

EPILOG: READYMADE CONTEMPORARY

MARCEL DUCHAMP: "But remember, I definitely do not want to create a school of the ready-made; far from it."
JEAN ANTOINE: "As a matter of fact, doesn't your concept of readymades preclude the idea of a school?"
MARCEL DUCHAMP: "Yes, to some extent, but not entirely. But, ultimately, I know there is an inherent danger in the readymade, and that is the ease with which it can be produced. So, if you were to create tens of thousands of readymades per year, that would become extremely monotonous and irritating. So I would recommend restraint in the production of readymades."[1] (Marcel Duchamp interviewed in 1965)

1 Jean Antoine, "An interview with Marcel Duchamp: 'I believe that a picture, a work of art, lives and dies just as we do...,'" *The Art Newspaper*, № 27, April 1993, online at: http://theartnewspaper.com/articles/An-interview-with-Marcel-Duchamp/29278.

Today the pluralism of artistic practices that include the "ready-made" have exploded long past the idea of limiting the number of readymades, which had been so crucial for Duchamp. When the artist pointed out in 1965 that he did not want to found a "school of the ready-made," he was conscious of the fact that this already had happened. From the 1960s up to now, we can compile a voluminous compendium of readymade-related works and artistic positions—as illustrated by a series of exhibitions covering the second half of the 20th century (see appendix for a list of exhibtions from the Duchamp centennial 1987 to the Readymade Centennial 2018).

As an ironic tribute to the countless variants and derivatives of Duchamp's readymades, John Armleder collected the *Readymades of the 20th Century* (1997–2000) in a kind of readymade *gesamtkunstwerk*. The main title of the work contains a warning to fellow artists and curators—*Don't do it!*—which expectedly remains without consequences: in the 21st century, too, we encounter ever more artistic practices that use the "already made."

The expansion of the readymade principle in recent art continues the pluralism, which was already part of Duchamp's work, and cannot be brought under a common denominator. Nevertheless, two strands can be discerned: on the one hand, the ongoing development of practices of the "already made" without an explicit reference to Duchamp's readymades; on the other, readymades *after* readymades, artistic references or revisions of Duchamp's works.

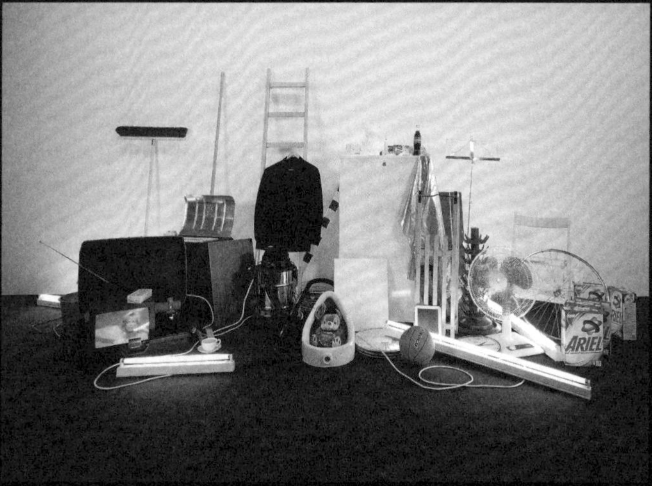

John Armleder, Don't do it! (Readymades of the 20th Century), *variable installation, top: 1997/2000, bottom: 1997/2011*

John Armleder: **Don't do it ! (Readymades of the 20th Century)**
F.S. (Furniture Sculpture) 1997/2000

Objekte	zitierte Künstler
Speichenrad	Duchamp
Flaschentrockner	Duchamp
Urinoir	Duchamp
Schneeschaufel	Duchamp
Koffer	Duchamp, Broodthaers, Beuys
Tasse	Meret Oppenheim
Schlitten	Beuys
Filz	Beuys, Robert Morris
Filmrollen	Beuys
ATA Scheuermittel	Beuys
Besen	Beuys, Man Ray
Schiefertafel	Beuys
Leiter	Beuys, Ruthenbeck, Herold
Anzug	Beuys, Broodthaers
CocaCola	Warhol
Campbells	Warhol
Dollarnote	Warhol
Waschpulver	Warhol, Haim Steinbach
Wasserball	Jeff Koons
Staubsauger	Jeff Koons, Wolf Vostell
Styroporbär	Jeff Koons
Plüschpuppe	Mike Kelley
Autoreifen	Alan Kaprow
Eimer	Robert Morris
Ventilator	Broodthaers, Bruce Nauman, McCaslin
Holzimitat	Richard Artschwager
Spiegel	Pistoletto, Gerhard Richter, Betrand Lavier
Kühlschrank	Bertrand Lavier
Stuhl	Rauschenberg, Kosuth, George Brecht
Fernseher	Nam June Paik, Wolf Vostell
Leuchtröhren	Dan Flavin
Uhr	Kosuth, Broodthaers, Rinke, McCaslin
Hammer	Man Ray, Uecker
Flasche	Man Ray, Broodthaers
Teller	Daniel Spoerri
Plastikgeschirr	Tony Cragg, Liptow
Schokolade	Dieter Roth
Hershey-Papier	Al Hansen
Plastikfolie	Christo
Goldstoff	James Lee Byars
Naturschwamm	Yves Klein
elektr. Zahnbürste	Richard Hamilton
Zollstock	Polke, Herold, Knoebel
Bilderrahmen	Knoebel
Rahmen m.Lwd	Paolini, Morellet
Arzneiverpackung	Damien Hirst
Teebeutel	Tiravanija

John Armleder, Don't do it! (Readymades of the 20th Century), *1997/2000, list of artists and objects*

The readymades *after* readymades by Sherrie Levine (*Fountain [After Duchamp]*, 1991) and Elaine Sturtevant (*Duchamp Fresh Widow*, 1992–2012) do not present ready-made objects that were selected by the artist, but, similar to Duchamp's multiples, they were produced in small limited-edition series to the artist's specifications and offered for sale on the art market. Interestingly, both artists, on different occasions, presented a complete edition of their multiples as temporary ensembles. Levine first showed *Fountain (After Duchamp)* in 1991 at Mary Boone Gallery, New York, with three copies from the edition of multiples simultaneously on view.[2] At the following museum exhibition in 1991–1992, the complete run of the six copies of the bronze sculptures were shown side by side.[3] Sturtevant exhibited the full edition of Duchamp's *Fresh Widow* (1992) in nine copies at the Moderna Museet Stockholm in 2012.[4] In these exhibitions, both Levine and Stur-

2 *Sherrie Levine: Fountain*, Mary Boone Gallery, New York 1991, catalog with a text by Bruce Ferguson. Cf. the review by Roberta Smith, "Art in Review," *New York Times*, May 24, 1991. Thanks to Grady O'Connor, David Zwirner Gallery, New York, for the suggestion.

3 *Sherrie Levine*, Kunsthalle Zürich 1991–1992, traveling to: Westfälisches Landesmuseum, Münster; Rooseum Center for Contemporary Art, Malmö; Hôtel des arts, Paris.

4 Elaine Sturtevant first produced

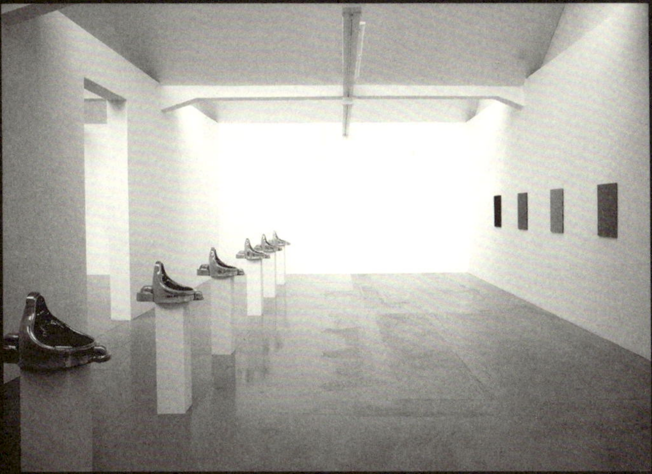

Sherry Levine, Fountain (After Duchamp), *1991 (sometimes titled* Fountain [Madonna]*)*

Edition of six multiples as an installation at Kunsthalle Zürich 1991

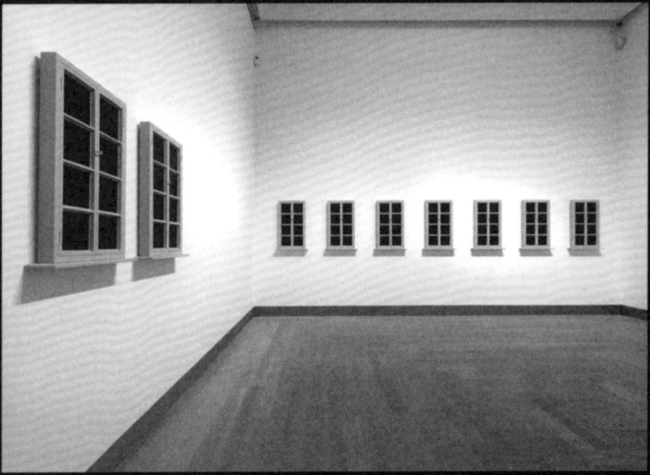

Elaine Sturtevant, Duchamp Fresh Widow, *1992–2012*

Edition of nine multiples as an installation at Moderna Museet Stockholm (where we also find the 1961 replica made by Ulf Linde and signed by Duchamp)

tevant presented the multiples as multiples (*after* readymades). Thus they countered the illusion of the singular readymade, which had established itself through the classic museum presentations of Duchamp's works. A similar effect in Duchamp's case would of course be possible if all eight copies of the multiple edition from 1964 were shown simultaneously.[5]

Duchamp Fresh Widow in 1992 as a replica, then in 2012 as an edition of nine copies for the exhibition *Sturtevant: Image over Image*, Moderna Museet, Stockholm 2012 (email to the author by Fredrik Liew, curator of the exhibition at Moderna Museet, June 1, 2016).

5 Germano Celant tried a comparable curatorial experiment when he exhibited several exemplars of the same object in his retrospective on the history of the multiple. He included two copies each from the 1964 edition of Duchamp's readymades as multiples (*The Small Utopia: Ars Multiplicata*, Fondazione Prada, Venice 2012). Four different versions of the *Bottle Dryer* were first shown together at the exhibition *Übrigens sterben immer die anderen: Marcel Duchamp und die Avantgarde seit 1950*, Museum Ludwig, Cologne 1988 (exhibition and catalog by Dieter Daniels and Alfred M. Fischer). The exhibition catalog for the first time illustrates as

As some copies were sold, the ensemble character soon dissolved after the exhibitions, and soon the multiples by Levine and Sturtevant were presented as unique exhibits just like Duchamp's readymades. While we have already discussed the aspect of Duchamp's post-readymades and Warhol's *Brillo Boxes* masking or respectively revealing the commodity status of the art "product," Levine's and Sturtevant's readymades *after* readymades give a whole new twist to the story: the art market's reinterpretation of the readymades now itself becomes a topic of artistic and also market-strategic "speculation," which moves us on to the next level of ambivalence between affirmation and critique.[6]

The historical process of the reception of the readymade principle and its various developments itself has become a theme for artistic approaches at the end of

much as eight different versions of the *Bottle Dryer*, each legitimized by the artist (ibid., pp. 78f). Contrary to the presentations of Levine, Sturtevant, and Celant, the exhibition and catalog clarified differences in form and size, to deconstruct the idea of the singular, self-identical object. (see illustration p. 118f in this book).

6 Cf. the panel discussion "Readymade Market" at the symposium *The Readymade Century* at Haus der Kulturen der Welt, Berlin, October 12–13, 2017, http://hkw.de/readymade.

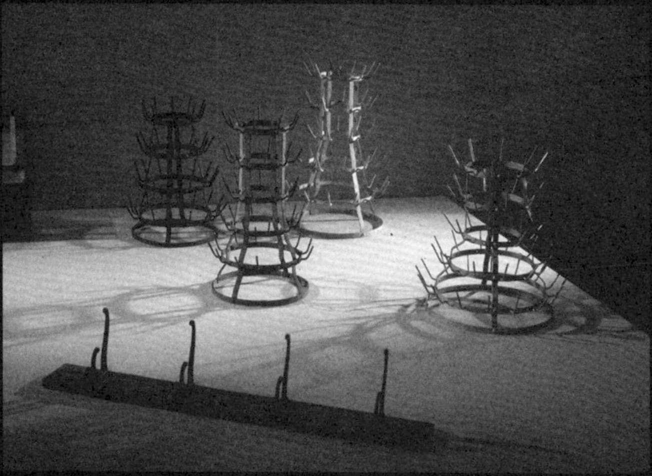

Constellation of three versions of the Bottle Dryer *signed by Duchamp (from 1921, 1960, and a multiple from 1964) as well as a new specimen from the Bazar de l'Hôtel de Ville in Paris, where Duchamp had bought his first Bottle Dryer in 1914*

Installation view at the exhibition Übrigens sterben immer die anderen: Marcel Duchamp und die Avantgarde seit 1950, *Museum Ludwig, Cologne 1988 (curators: Dieter Daniels and Alfred M. Fischer)*

the “Readymade Century.” The conflict between singularity and pluralism, which has already been laid out in Duchamp’s work, is explored e.g. in ensembles by Bethan Huws and Saâdane Afif.

Huws presents an installation of 88 bottle dryers in different sizes and forms under the suggestive title *Forest* (2008–2009).[7] As an ensemble of meta-readymades, *Forest* evokes Duchamp’s lost object while making it disappear behind gradations of differences. Their patina and clear signs of usage lend each of the pieces a sense of its own story and individuality, and so they become objects of contemplation. In this sense, *Forest* deliberately contradicts Duchamp’s quest for an aesthetic indifference.[8]

With his *Fountain Archives* (2008–2017), Saâdane Afif has built an “imaginary museum” of reproductions, which will finally comprise 1001 images of the titular readymade collected from various publications.[9] This archive, organized after a strictly scientific classification system, reflects the wide distribution of Duchamp’s

7 Bethan Huws, *Forest*, Cologne 2015 (exhibition at Staatliche Kunsthalle, Karlsruhe 2015–2016).

8 Bethan Huws comments: “The difficulty of doing anything ‘new’ in the sense that always ‘something’ is pre-existing—we make the ‘new’ from the ‘old.’” (Conversation with the author, Berlin, December 3, 2016.)

9 See: http://thefountainarchives.net; Saâdane Afif, *Fontaines*, Brussels 2014.

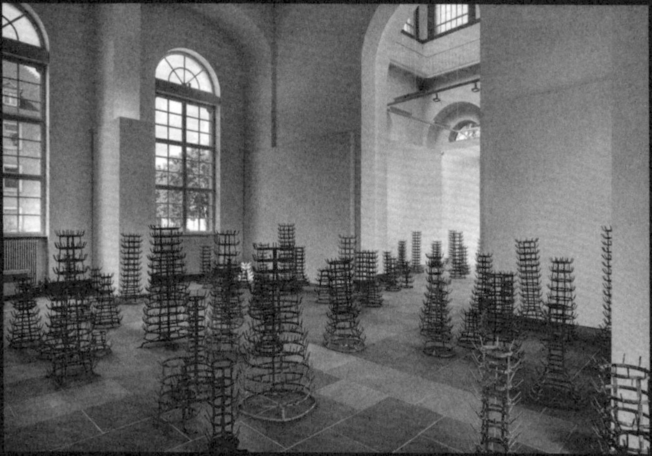

Bethan Huws, Forest, *2008–2009 (exhibition at Staatliche Kunsthalle, Karlsruhe 2015)*

Fountain, which today has become an icon of modernism. At the same time, the visible differences between the objects and their modes of representation within the illustrations reinforce the absurdity of a search for their "authentic" (pre-)image or origin.

The Fountain Archives portray the "Readymade Century" as a century of reproduction: a urinal that was never exhibited, that was soon lost and rarely photographed, has caused a steadily growing avalanche of illustrations. On a second layer, this process also takes hold of Saâdane Afif's own artistic project: any published appraisal of the *Fountain Archives* leads to a growing number of illustrations from the project, and the *Fountain Archives* themselves become a component of itself, the *Fountain Archives*, occupying a specially created „augmented" section within them.[10]

These "epistemic" constellations in the work of Bethan Huws and Saâdane Afif play on the difference between the imaginary (the readymade, which according to Duchamp need not be looked at, whose existence must be known but offers nothing to the contemplative gaze) and the real (facts of the objects and differences between the objects that can only be seen in actual com-

10 Hence this book will also become part of the "augmented" section. In this case the illustration reproduced on p. 154, where Ridvan Askin's book shows a page from Arturo Schwarz's Complete Works, will enter the Fountain Archives for the third time, as a reproduction of a reproduction of a reproduction.

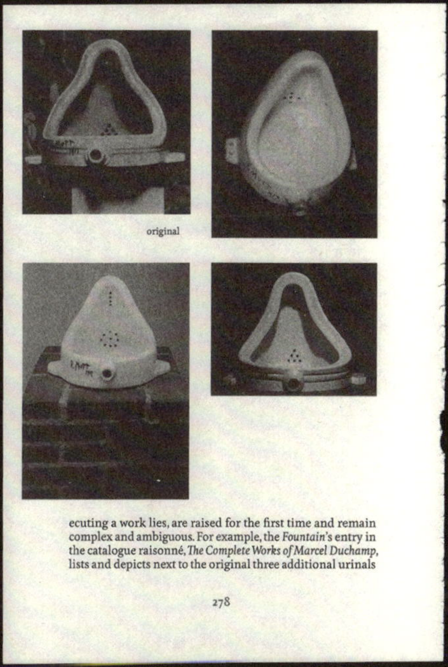

original

ecuting a work lies, are raised for the first time and remain complex and ambiguous. For example, the *Fountain*'s entry in the catalogue raisonné, *The Complete Works of Marcel Duchamp*, lists and depicts next to the original three additional urinals

278

Saâdane Afif, The Fountain Archives FA.0489, *2015*

Torn out page from: Askin, Ridvan et al. (eds). Speculations V: Aesthetics in the 21st Century. *New York: Punctum Books, 2014—p. 278*

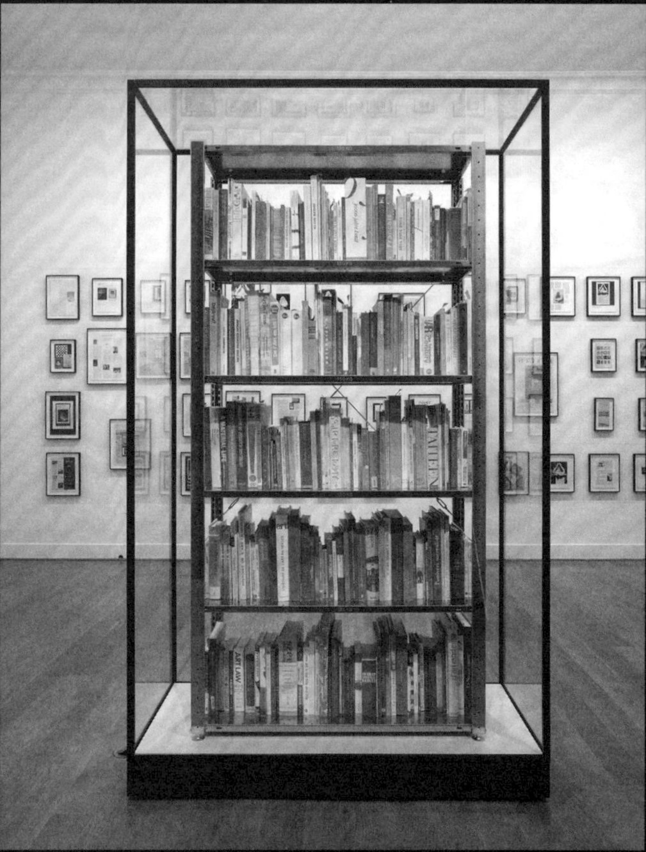

Saâdane Afif, The Fountain Archives 2008–2017

Exhibition view Nouveau Musée National de Monaco—Villa Sauber

parison). Their work thematizes the idolization and fictionalization of Duchamp's readymades during the history of their reception as well as the intangibility of a supposed "original," which recedes further and further with its multiplications.

Most of the practices of the "already made" today do not explicitly refer to Duchamp's readymades, but to aspects of our contemporary art world and commodity culture. So what shifts in meaning do we find in the concepts of the "contemporary readymade" under the post-modern, post-colonial, and post-medial conditions of a "post-contemporary art"?[11] The (post-)contemporary readymade does not form another genre in the classical canon of the arts, but instead a cross-disciplinary method or approach, which offers new principles of authorship and originality on a level with already established forms. The huge diversification and dilation of the readymade principle a hundred years after Duchamp seems to be based on the historical openness of the term, on this indefinability that we have

11 On the term "post-contemporary" see the *Post-contemporary* issue of *Dis Magazine* (April 2016), edited by Armen Avanessian and Suhail Malik, http://dismagazine.com/issues/post-contemporary; cf. also Armen Avanessian and Suhail Malik, "The Time-Complex. Postcontemporary," *Fear of Content*, IX. Berlin Biennale 2016, http://bb9.berlinbiennale.de/the-time-complex-postcontemporary.

discussed at some length, which allows for a constant updating and expansion.

Circulation of capital, globalization of markets, establishing transnational brand identities, and the new (post-)industrial processes for manufacturing goods—these are central themes of artistic practices that revisit the readymade in the 21st century. Art becomes part of a feedback loop: on the one hand it explores or critiques the global circulation of goods and "cognitive capitalism," on the other it serves the market capitalization of ideas and brands by "re-branding the readymade" (Martha Buskirk) as art merchandise.[12]

With this we can finally see another reason for the currentness of the readymade, reaching far beyond Duchamp's work: the continuing state of tension between the two meanings of the word ready-made / readymade, between industrial and artistic production—or, more generally, between the unabated need for individuality and the formatting of that need by the capitalist production of commodities, ever progressing since Duchamp's time.

This culturohistorical dimension also sees the readymade as a witness of its time: *Every readymade was or is "contemporary" by its very essence: it is like a snapshot of the time of its selection, which contrasts with*

12 See: Martha Buskirk, *Creative Enterprise: Contemporary Art between Museum and Marketplace*, New York 2012, pp. 201–262.

the timelessness of artworks in the classic genres.[13] The significance of Duchamp's readymades, as well as that of today's practices, evolving independently, is not limited to the sphere of art. Instead these practices are "externalizing a way of viewing the world" and "expressing the interior of a cultural period," as Arthur C. Danto has written in reference to the *Brillo Boxes.*[14] This is what we talk about when we speak of a "Readymade Century." And it is the main reason why it is still fascinating to again reconsider Duchamp's readymades after a hundred years.[15]

13 From this perspective, we might also reconsider Duchamp's own readymades as witnesses of their time. So far it has hardly been recognized that the period of creation for the original readymades largely coincided with the First World War, which was also the reason why Duchamp moved from Paris to New York (see Hadrien Laroche, *Duchamp déchets: Les hommes, les objets, la catastrophe*, Paris 2014).

14 Danto, *The Transfiguration of the Commonplace*, p. 208.

15 The currentness of the readymade principle in contemporary art was discussed in a symposium curated by the author: *The Readymade Century* at Haus der Kulturen der Welt, Berlin, October 12–13, 2017, see: http://hkw.de/readymade.

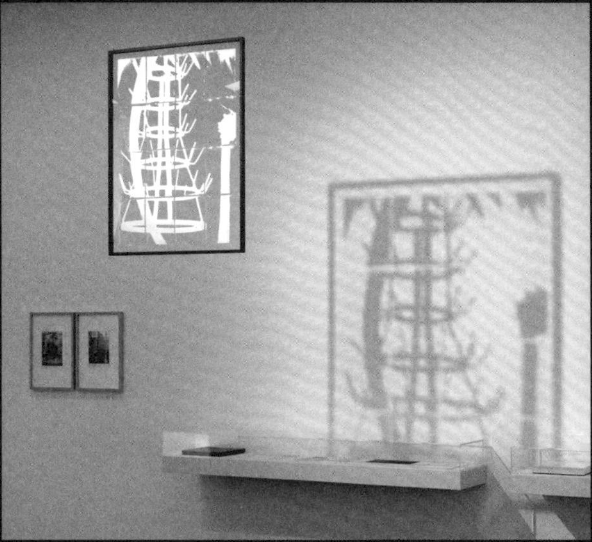

Marcel Duchamp, Suite d'ombres transparents, *1967*

16 silkscreens in white on acetate foil, in: Octavio Paz, Marcel Duchamp ou le Château de la Pureté, *Paris 1967*

The silkscreen is based on the photograph of the shadow of the multiple of the Bottle Dryer. *Thus the shadow on the wall is a shadow of the printed shadow, such as the 1964 multiple is an afterimage of the photograph taken by Man Ray from the 1936 replica, which is an afterimage of the lost 1914* Bottle Dryer. *So what we see on the wall is the afterimage of an afterimage of an afterimage of an afterimage of an afterimage of an afterimage.*

I. READYMADE READINGS

MARCEL DUCHAMP BASICS: BOXES / BOÎTES

Marcel Duchamp, *The Bride Stripped Bare by Her Bachelors, Even*. A typographic version by Richard Hamilton of Marcel Duchamp's Green Box. Translated by George Heard Hamilton, Edition Hansjörg Mayer, Stuttgart / London / Reykjavik 3rd ed. 1976

Marcel Duchamp, *A l'infinitif.* A typotranslation by Richard Hamilton and Ecke Bonk of Marcel Duchamp's White Box, Northend Chapter 1999

Ecke Bonk, *The Box in a Valise*: *de ou par Marcel Duchamp ou Rrose Selavy*: inventory of an edition; translated by David Britt, New York 1989

De ou par Marcel Duchamp ou Rrose Sélavy (*Boîte-en-valise*) / *From or by Marcel Duchamp or Rrose Sélavy* (*Box in a Valise*), Facsimile of the G 1968 edition, edited by Mathieu Mercier and Verlag der Buchhandlung Walther König, Cologne 2016

MARCEL DUCHAMP BASICS: WORKS / WRITINGS / CORRESPONDENCE

Schwarz, Arturo, *The complete works of Marcel Duchamp*, New York 2000 (revised and expanded paperback edition, first edition: 1969)

Michel Sanouillet and Elmer Peterson (eds.), *The Writings of Marcel Duchamp*, New York 1989 (first edition: 1973)

Marcel Duchamp, *Notes*, preface by Pontus Hultén, presentation and translation by Paul Matisse,

Paris, Centre National d'Art et de Culture Centre Pompidou, 1980 (posthumously published notes)
Francis M. Naumann and Hector Obalk (eds.), *Affectt Marcel: The Selected Correspondence of Marcel Duchamp*, London 2000

MARCEL DUCHAMP INTERVIEWS AND STATEMENTS (CHRONOLOGICAL AFTER DATE OF INTERVIEW 1959–1968, SELECTED BY RELEVANCE FOR THE READYMADE)

Hamilton / Hamilton 1959: George Heard Hamilton and Richard Hamilton, "Marcel Duchamp Speaks," (radio interview BBC—Third Program, series: Art, Anti-Art, ca. October 1959); issued as an audio tape by William Furlong (ed.), *Audio Arts Magazine*, vol. 2, № 4, 1976 (London), audio online: http://tate.org.uk/audio-arts/volume-2/number-4
Duchamp 1961: Marcel Duchamp, "Apropos of 'Readymades'," lecture at the symposium *The Art of Assemblage*, Museum of Modern Art, New York, October 19, 1961, first printed in: *Art and Artists*, London, vol. I, № 4, July 1966, p. 47
Charbonnier 1960–61: Georges Charbonnier, *Entretiens avec Marcel Duchamp*, Paris 1994, published also on audio CD by André Dimanche, 1994 (six radio interviews, RTF France Culture, 1960–1961), audio online: https://youtu.be/1gNqeNNPkOs
Kuh 1961: Katherine Kuh, Marcel Duchamp, in: *The Artist's Voice. Talks with Seventeen Modern Artists*, New York 1962, p. 81–93 (BBC radio interview 1961)

Roberts 1963: Francis Roberts, “I Propose to Strain the Laws of Physics,” *Art News*, vol. 67, № 8, December 1968, p. 46–47, 62–64 (magazine interview 1963)

Tomkins 1964: Calvin Tomkins, *Marcel Duchamp: The Afternoon Interviews*, New York 2013 (interviews 1964)

Friedman 1965: Marcel Duchamp talking about the readymade with Martin Friedman (public museum talk, October 18, 1965) Conversation not yet transcribed, audio as part of a video from the Walker Art Center, 2012, video online: https://youtu.be/VYqDpNmnu8I

Neyens 1965: Interview with Marcel Duchamp by Jean Neyens for RTBF in 1965. English translation: tout-fait vol. 2, issue 4 [2002]; http://toutfait.com/issues/volume2/issue_4/interviews/md_jean/md_jean.html

Hahn 1966 a: Otto Hahn, “Passport No. G255300,” in: *Art and Artists*, London, vol. I, № 4, July 1966, pp. 7–11 (magazine interview in French with Otto Hahn 1966, translated by Andrew Rabeneck)

Hahn 1966 b: “Marcel Duchamp” in: *VH 101*, № 3, Paris 1970, p. 54–61 (magazine interview in French with Otto Hahn 1966)

Cabanne 1967: Pierre Cabanne, *Entretiens avec Marcel Duchamp*, Paris 2014 (first edition: 1967, first english edition: Pierre Cabanne, *Dialogues with Marcel Duchamp*, London 1971)

Collin 1967: "Marcel Duchamp Talking about Readymades," Interview with Philippe Collin, in: *Marcel Duchamp*, ed. by Museum Jean Tinguely, Basel, Ostfildern 2002, pp. 37–41 (interview Radiodiffusion Telévision Française, 1967)

Antoine 1967: Jean Antoine, "An interview with Marcel Duchamp: 'I believe that a picture, a work of art, lives and dies just as we do...,'" *The Art Newspaper*, № 27, April 1993, (television interview 1967, broadcast RTB 1971), video online: http://jean-antoine.com/marcel-duchamp

Bakewell 1968: "The Late Show Line Up: Interview with Marcel Duchamp by Joan Bakewell," in: Francis M. Naumann, *Marcel Duchamp: The Art of Making Art in the Age of Mechanical Reproduction*, Ghent and New York 1999, p. 304 (television interview BBC Two, 1968), video online: http://bbc.co.uk/programmes/p04826th

HISTORIC SOURCES (CHRONOLOGICAL 1916–1938, SELECTED BY RELEVANCE FOR THE READYMADE)

Katherine S. Dreier Papers, Beinecke Rare Book & Manuscript Library, Yale University

Nixola Greeley-Smith, "Cubist Depicts Love in Brass and Glass," *The Evening World*, April 4, 1916, reprinted in: Rudolf E. Kuenzli (ed.), New York Dada, New York 1986, pp. 135–137

The Blind Man, P.T.B., № 2, May 1917 (ed. Beatrice Wood, in collaboration with Henri-Pierre Roché and Marcel Duchamp, both uncredited)

William Carlos Williams, "Dialogue: The Return of

the Sun," in: *The Little Review*, vol. 5, № 11 [12], April 1919, pp. 1–10

André Breton, "Marcel Duchamp," in: *Litterature*, n.s. № 5, 1922, pp. 7–10. English translation in: Motherwell, Robert (ed.), The Dada Painters and Poets, New York 1951

Katherine S. Dreier, *Western Art and the New Era*, New York 1923

Georges Hugnet, "L'Esprit Dada dans la peinture" (part 1), in: *Cahiers d'Art*, № 1, 1932, pp. 57–65

André Breton, "Phare de la mariée," in: *Minotaure*, № 6, winter 1934 / 35, pp. 45–49. English translation: André Breton, "Lighthouse of the Bride," in: *View. The Modern Magazine*, Marcel Duchamp Number, series V, № 1, 1945

Gabriële Buffet, "Coeurs volants," in: *Cahiers d'Art*, nos. 1–2, 1936, pp. 34–43. English translation: *View. The Modern Magazine* 1945

André Breton and Paul Éluard (eds.), *Dictionnaire abrégé du Surréalisme*, Paris 1938, entry: Readymade, p. 23

RECOMMENDED RECENT READINGS (SINCE 2010, ALPHABETICAL ORDER)

Stefan Banz, *Marcel Duchamp: Pharmacie*, Nuremberg 2013

Lars Blunck, *Marcel Duchamp: Porte-bouteilles*, Nuremberg 2014

Lars Blunck, *Duchamps Readymade*, Munich 2017

Martha Buskirk, *Creative Enterprise: Contemporary Art between Museum and Marketplace*, New York 2012

Jaimey Hamilton Faris, *Uncommon Goods: Global Dimensions of the Readymade*, Chicago 2013

Maurizio Lazzarato, *Marcel Duchamp and The Refusal of Work*, Los Angeles CA 2014

Thomas Girst, *The Duchamp Dictionary*, London 2014 (entries: Edition of 1964–65, Readymade, Rendezvous, Replica)

Elena Filipovic, *The Apparently Marginal Activities of Marcel Duchamp*, Cambridge, MA, and London 2016

Paul B. Franklin "Exposing Duchamp in Sweden," in: *Étant donné*, № 11, Paris 2016, pp. 94–141

Hadrien Laroche, *Duchamp déchets: Les hommes, les objets, la catastrophe*, Paris 2014

Herbert Molderings, *Duchamp and the Aesthetics of Chance: Art as Experiment*, Columbia University Press New York, 2010

Subsequent to this book having been already completed, Adina Kamien-Kazhdan published her—in many ways complementary and in some aspects contradictory—study on the readymade multiples and on the collaboration of Marcel Duchamp and Arturo Schwarz: *Remaking the Readymade: Duchamp, Man Ray, and the Conundrum of the Replica*, Routledge London / New York, 2018

II. LEGACY OF THE READYMADE

EXHIBITIONS AND CATALOGS (CHRONOLOGICAL 1988–2018)

Übrigens sterben immer die anderen: Marcel Duchamp und die Avantgarde seit 1950, Museum Ludwig, Cologne 1988 [curated by Dieter Daniels and Alfred M. Fischer]

The Readymade Boomerang: Certain Relations in 20th Century Art (8th Biennale of Sydney), Art Gallery of New South Wales, Sydney 1990 [curated by René Block]

Das Jahrhundert des Multiple—Von Duchamp bis zur Gegenwart, Deichtorhallen, Hamburg 1994 [curated by Zdenek Felix]

Dinge in der Kunst des XX. Jahrhunderts, Haus der Kunst, Munich 2000 [curated by Hubertus Gaßner and Stephanie Rosenthal]

Marcel Duchamp, Museum Jean Tinguely Basel, 2002 [curated by Harald Szeemann]

Nichts weiter als ein Rendezvous, Künstlerhaus Bremen, 2007 [curated by Susanne Pfeffer]

Re-Object: Marcel Duchamp, Damien Hirst, Jeff Koons, Gerhard Merz, Kunsthaus Bregenz, 2007 [curated by Eckhard Schneider]

An Unruly History of the Readymade, Fundación / Colección Jumex, Mexico, 2008 [curated by Jessica Morgan]

After the Readymade, University of Chicago, Smart Museum of Art 2010 [curated by Emily Capper, Christine Mehring, no catalog]

New Realisms: 1957–1962: Object Strategies between Readymade and Spectacle, Museo Reina Sofía, Madrid 2010 [curated by Julia Robinson]

It Is What It Is. Or Is It?, Contemporary Art Museum Houston 2012 [curated by Dean Daderko]

Tell Me Whom You Haunt: Marcel Duchamp and the Contemporary Readymade, Blain|Southern Gallery, London 2013 [no catalog]

Picasso/Duchamp "He Was Wrong," Moderna Museet, Stockholm 2012 [curated by Daniel Birnbaum, Ronald Jones, Annika Gunnarsson]

The Small Utopia: Ars Multiplicata, Fondazione Prada, Venice 2012 [curated by Germano Celant]

Dancing Around the Bride: Cage, Cunningham, Johns, Rauschenberg, and Duchamp, Philadephia Museum of Art, 2012 [curated by Carlos Basualdo]

Reinventing the Wheel: The Readymade Century, Monash University Museum of Art, Melbourne 2013 [curated by Charlotte Day, Robert Leonard, no catalog]

Duchamp: Re-made in Italy, La Galleria Nazionale d'Arte Moderna, Rome 2013 [curated by Stefano Cecchetto, Giovanna Coltelli, Marcella Cossu]

Marcel Duchamp, Gagosian Gallery, New York 2014 [readymade multiples, catalog with contributions by Calvin Tomkins, Adina Kamien-Kazhdan]

What Marcel Duchamp Taught Me, The Fine Art Society, London 2014 [no catalog]

Julian Wasser: Duchamp in Pasadena Revisited, E6 Gallery, San Francisco 2015 [no catalog]

Julian Wasser: Duchamp in Pasadena Redux, Robert Berman Gallery, Los Angeles 2016 [no catalog]

Der Duchamp Effekt. Readymade. Werke aus der Daimler Art Collection, Kunsthalle Göppingen 2016 [curated by Renate Wiehager, Werner Meyer, Melanie Ardjah, no catalog]

No Place Like Home, The Israel Museum, Jerusalem, Bella and Harry Wexner Gallery 2017 [curated by Adina Kamien-Kazhdan]

Marcel Duchamp—Porte-bouteilles, Galerie Thaddaeus Ropac (Marais), Paris 2017 [catalog with contributions by Cécile Debray, Paul B. Franklin]

Ramon Haze—Der Schrank / The Cabinet (1997–2017), KOW Gallery, Berlin 2017 [no catalog]

Some Aesthetic Decisions: A Centennial Celebration of Marcel Duchamp's Fountain, NSU Art Museum Fort Lauderdale, 2017 [curated by Bonnie Clearwater]

Marcel Duchamp Fountain: An Homage, Francis M. Naumann Fine Art, 2017 [curated by Francis M. Naumann]

Marcel Duchamp and the Fountain Scandal, Philadelphia Museum of Art, 2017 [curated by Matthew Affron, John Vick]

Marcel Duchamp. 100 Questions. 100 Answers, Staatsgalerie Stuttgart, 2018 [curated by Susanne M.I. Kaufmann]

READYMADE CENTENNIAL: CONFERENCES (2015–2018)

The Readymade Century revisited, Lecture Series: *The Creative Imperative*, Cooperation between

Stedelijk Museum Amsterdam and VU University Amsterdam, Stedelijk Museum Amsterdam, November 12, 2015, Contributions by Dieter Daniels and Jonas Lund. Video (in English): https://vimeo.com/147591899

100 Jahre Readymade. How to make a readymade?, Staatliche Kunsthalle Karlsruhe, January 16, 2016 Contributions by Dieter Daniels and Lars Blunk. Videos (in German): https://youtu.be/zlQULZYB7tM, https://youtu.be/yzh1T_mDFPw

100 years after / the readymade, HGB Leipzig, June 9, 2016, conference curated by Dieter Daniels with contributions by Lars Blunck, Dieter Daniels, Peter Piller, Wolfgang Ullrich, Benjamin Meyer-Krahmer, Barbara Steiner.
Video Archive (in German): https://youtu.be/yTrd4c9xBJ0

The Readymade Century, International Symposium, HKW, Haus der Kulturen der Welt, Berlin, October 12–13, 2017, curated by Dieter Daniels in collaboration with Annette Bhagwati.
With contributions by Saâdane Afif, Inke Arns, Kader Attia, Annette Bhagwati, Lars Blunck, Martha Buskirk, Dieter Daniels, Simon Denny, Sebastian Egenhofer, Famed (Sebastian Kretzschmar, Jan Thomaneck), Thomas Girst, Isabelle Graw, Katja Kwastek, Oliver Laric, Sven Lütticken, Benjamin Meyer-Krahmer, Olaf Nicolai, Margareta von Oswald, Matthew Plummer-Fernandez, Annette Tietenberg, Gesine Tosin, Tobias Vogt. Program: https://hkw.de/en/programm/projekte/2017/the_ready_made_

century/the_ready_made_century_start.php. Video Archive (in English): https://hkw.de/de/app/mediathek/project/134963-the-ready-made-century

Duchamp's Readymades: A Reevaluation, International Symposium, Aarhus University, May 31–June 1, 2018 curated by Jakob Wamberg, with contributions by Linda Dalrymple Henderson, Thierry de Duve, David Joselit, Sarah Kolb, Thomas Girst, Glyn Thompson, Dieter Daniels, Jacob Wamberg. Program: http://events.au.dk/readymades2018. Proceedings will be published in the Nordic Journal of Aesthetics, https://tidsskrift.dk/nja

IMAGE CREDITS

Cover: Marcel Duchamp, *Suite d'ombres transparents*, 1967. 16 silkscreens in white on acetate foil, in: Octavio Paz, *Marcel Duchamp ou le Château de la Pureté*, Paris 1967
Photo: Rheinisches Bildarchiv, Köln, 1988 © Rheinisches Bildarchiv;
Artwork: © Association Marcel Duchamp / VG Bild-Kunst, Bonn, 2018

Insert in Cover front: Photo: archive of the author

Insert in Cover back: Photo: Daniels, Dieter, 2012 © Dieter Daniels

p. 8: Photos: Daniels, Dieter, 2015 © Dieter Daniels

pp. 17–18: Photos: Archives of American Art, Smithsonian Institution, Washington DC. © Archives of American Art, Smithsonian Institution, Washington DC.

p. 20: Photo top: archive of the author
Photo bottom: archive of the author © The New York Sun, New York

p. 23: Photo: The International Dada Archive at the University of Iowa Libraries, 2012 © University of Iowa;
Artwork: © Association Marcel Duchamp / VG Bild-Kunst, Bonn, 2018

p. 25: Photo: Daniels, Dieter, 2018 © Dieter Daniels
Artwork: © Association Marcel Duchamp / VG Bild-Kunst, Bonn, 2018

p. 26: Photo: Philadelphia Museum of Art © Philadelphia Museum of Art
Artwork: © Association Marcel Duchamp / VG Bild-Kunst, Bonn, 2018

p. 30: Photo: Kunstmuseum Liechtenstein, 2016 © Kunstmuseum Liechtenstein
Artwork: © Association Marcel Duchamp / VG Bild-Kunst, Bonn, 2018

pp. 33–35: Photos: Staatsgalerie Stuttgart, 2018 © Staatsgalerie Stuttgart
Artworks: © Association Marcel Duchamp / VG Bild-Kunst, Bonn, 2018

p. 36: Photos: Kunstmuseum Liechtenstein, 2016 © Kunstmuseum Liechtenstein
Artwork: © Association Marcel Duchamp / VG Bild-Kunst, Bonn, 2018

p. 37: Photo top: Philadelphia Museum of Art © Philadelphia Museum of Art
Photo middle: Staatsgalerie Stuttgart, 2018 © Staatsgalerie Stuttgart
Photo bottom: Staatliches Museum Schwerin © Staatliches Museum Schwerin
Artworks: © Association Marcel Duchamp / VG Bild-Kunst, Bonn, 2018

p. 39: Photo: Mulas, Ugo, © Estate of Ugo Mulas (reproduced in: *Étant donné*, № 11, Paris 2016, p. 128)

p. 40: Illustration from: Walter Hopps; Ulf Linde; Arturo Schwarz; *Marcel Duchamp: Ready-mades, etc. (1913–1964)*, Galleria Schwarz, Milan and Le Terrain Vague, Paris 1964.

p. 46: Illustration from: *Art and Artists*, vol. I, № 4 (July 1966), p. 47 © Art and Artists
Text: © Association Marcel Duchamp
p. 48: Photo: Daniels, Dieter, 2015 © Dieter Daniels
Artwork: © Association Marcel Duchamp
p. 53: Photo: Philadelphia Museum of Art
© Philadelphia Museum of Art
Text: © Association Marcel Duchamp
p. 55: Photo: Staatsgalerie Stuttgart, 2018
© Staatsgalerie Stuttgart
p. 84: Photo: Rheinisches Bildarchiv, Köln 1988
© Rheinisches Bildarchiv
p. 94: Top: Illustration from: *Phaidon Encyclopedia of Art and Artists*, London 1978, p. 148
© Phaidon Press, 1978
Bottom: Illustration from: *BBC One Minute World News*, 1. December 2004 © BBC World News, 2004
p. 102: Photo: Roché, Henri-Pierre (attributed)
© Philadelphia Museum of Art, Gift of Jacqueline, Paul, and Peter Matisse in memory of their mother, Alexina Duchamp, 1998
p. 104: Photo: Baker, Oliver 1953 © Archives of American Art, Smithsonian Institution, Washington DC. (reproduced in: William Camfield, *Marcel Duchamp. Fountain*, Houston 1989, p. 81)
p. 108: Photo top: Rheinisches Bildarchiv, Köln 1988
© Rheinisches Bildarchiv
Photo bottom: reproduced in Elena Filipovic, *A Museum That is Not*, 2009 p. 6
Artworks: © Association Marcel Duchamp / VG Bild-Kunst, Bonn 2018
p. 110: Photo: Thomas, Frank J. © Frank J. Thomas

Archives (reproduced in: William Camfield, *Marcel Duchamp. Fountain*, Houston 1989, p. 108)

pp. 113–114: Illustration from: Dieter Daniels and Alfred M. Fischer, *Übrigens sterben immer die anderen: Marcel Duchamp und die Avantgarde seit 1950*, Museum Ludwig, Cologne 1988, pp. 78–79
© Dieter Daniels and Alfred M. Fischer / Museum Ludwig, Cologne

p. 117: Illustration from: Arturo Schwarz, *The Complete Works of Marcel Duchamp*, Delano Grenidge press, New York 2000; No. 345
© Arturo Schwarz / Delano Grenidge press

p. 119: Photo: Courtesy Association Marcel Duchamp
Artwork: © Association Marcel Duchamp / VG Bild-Kunst, Bonn, 2018

p. 120: Photo: Courtesy Association Marcel Duchamp
Artworks © Association Marcel Duchamp / VG Bild-Kunst, Bonn, 2018

p. 123: Photo: Umbo (Otto Umbehr), 1965
© Sprengel-Museum in Hannover / Kestner Gesellschaft Hannover

p. 126: Photo: Mulas, Ugo, 1964 © Estate of Ugo Mulas

p. 127: Photo: Umbo (Otto Umbehr), 1965
© Sprengel-Museum in Hannover / Kestner Gesellschaft Hannover

p. 130: Photo: McDarrah, Fred W., 1964 © Estate of Fred W. McDarrah (reproduced in: David Bourdon, *Andy Warhol*, DuMont Verlag, Köln 1989, p. 171)

p. 133: Illustrations from: *Duchamp: Re-made in Italy*, La Galleria Nazionale d'Arte Moderna, 2013 pp. 144–145 © Carlo Scarpa estate

p. 137: Photo: Staatliches Museum Schwerin
© Staatliches Museum Schwerin
Artwork: © Association Marcel Duchamp / VG Bild-Kunst, Bonn 2018

p. 141: Photo top: Courtesy Galerie Anselm Dreher, Berlin, 2000
Photo bottom: Courtesy Galerie Bruno Bischofberger, Zurich, 2011
Artworks: © John Armleder

p. 142: Photo: Courtesy Galerie Anselm Dreher, Berlin
Artwork: Armleder, John, 2000 © John Armleder

p. 144: Photo: Troehler, Alexander, 1991 © Alexander Troehler
Artwork: Levine, Sherrie, 1991 © Sherrie Levine

p. 145: Photo: Courtesy of Moderna Museet Stockholm
© Moderna Museet Stockholm
Artwork: Sturtevant, Elaine, 1992 © Elaine Sturtevant

p. 148: Photo: Daniels, Dieter, 1988 © Dieter Daniels

p. 150: Photo: Courtesy of Staatliche Kunsthalle, Karlsruhe, 2015
Artwork: Huws, Bethan, 2008–2009 © Bethan Huws

p. 152: Photo: Courtesy of Afif, Saâdane
© Saâdane Afif

p. 153: Photo: NMNM / François Fernandez, 2017
NMNM / François Fernandez
Artworks: Afif, Saâdane, 2017 © Saâdane Afif

p. 159: Photo: Kunstmuseum Liechtenstein, 2016
© Kunstmuseum Liechtenstein
Artwork: © Association Marcel Duchamp / VG Bild-Kunst, Bonn, 2018

p. 186: Photo: Kunstmuseum Liechtenstein, 2016
© Kunstmuseum Liechtenstein
Artwork: © Association Marcel Duchamp / VG Bild-Kunst, Bonn, 2018

Despite intensive research, it has not always been possible to identify all copyright holders. We kindly ask for your understanding, should we not have respected individual authors.

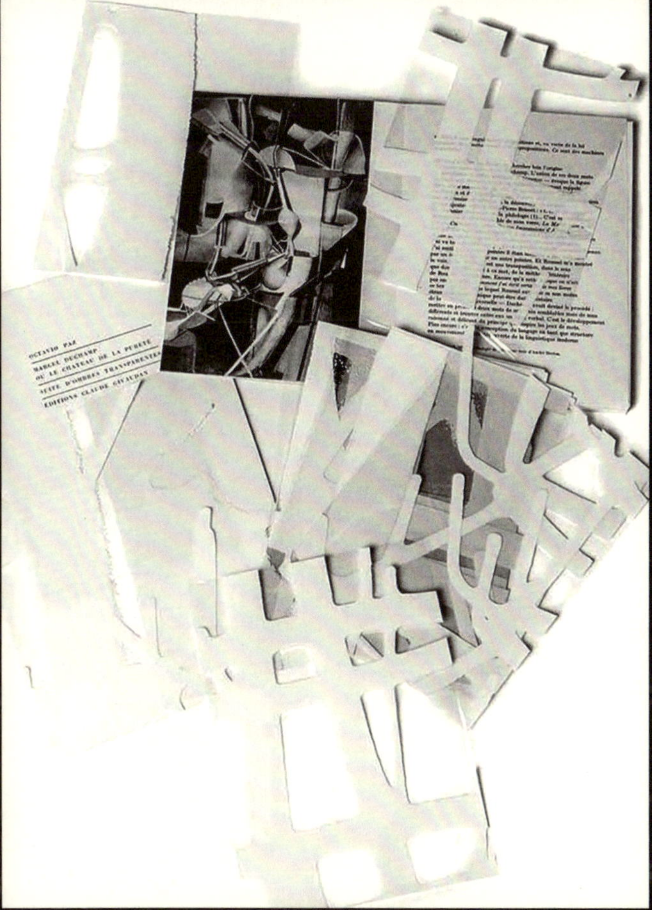

Marcel Duchamp, Suite d'ombres transparents, *1967*

16 silkscreens in white on acetate foil, in: Octavio Paz, Marcel Duchamp ou le Château de la Pureté, *Paris 1967*

Dieter Daniels, Readymade Century
with a contribution by Olaf Nicolai

Concept, graphic design, typesetting: Dan Solbach,
with Megan Dieudonné
Translation: Lutz Eitel
Copyediting: Jan-Frederik Bandel, Ames Gerould
Proofreading: Ames Gerould
Typefaces: Display Grotesk (Chi-Long Trieu),
Untitled Sans & Serif (Kris Sowersby)
Printing: Druckhaus Köthen

Published by
Spector Books
Harkortstraße 10, 04107 Leipzig, spectorbooks.com

Distribution:
Germany, Austria: GVA, Gemeinsame Verlagsauslieferung Göttingen GmbH & Co. KG, http://gva-verlage.de
Switzerland: AVA Verlagsauslieferung AG, http://ava.ch
France, Belgium: Interart Paris, http://interart.fr
UK: Central Books Ltd, http://centralbooks.com
USA, Canada, Central and South America, Africa, Asia: ARTBOOK / D.A.P., http://artbook.com
South Korea: The Book Society, thebooksociety.org
Australia, New Zealand: Perimeter Distribution, http://perimeterdistribution.com

The German version of this book was also published by Spector Books. ISBN: 978-3-95905-132-3

First edition
ISBN 978-3-95905-139-2

Printed in Germany